# BEST OF TAL FARLOW

Music transcriptions by Pete Billmann, Aurélien Budynek, Paul Pappas, and Martin Shellard

Cover photo © Metronome/Getty Images

ISBN 978-1-4803-8368-5

HAL•LEONARD®
CORPORATION
7777 W. BLUEMOUND RD. P.O. BOX 13819 MILWAUKEE, WI 53213

Visit Hal Leonard Online at
**www.halleonard.com**

from *Chromatic Palette*

# All Alone
## Words and Music by Irving Berlin

**A**

**Very fast** ♩ = 264 ( ♪♪ = ♪♪ )

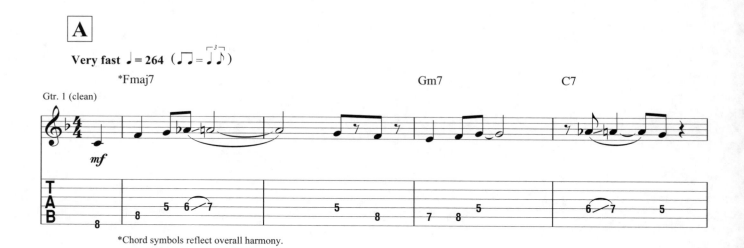

*Chord symbols reflect overall harmony.

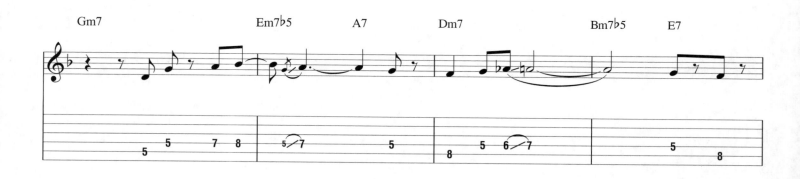

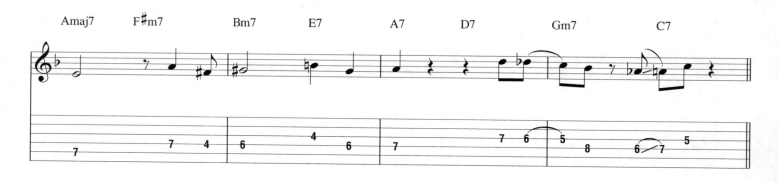

3

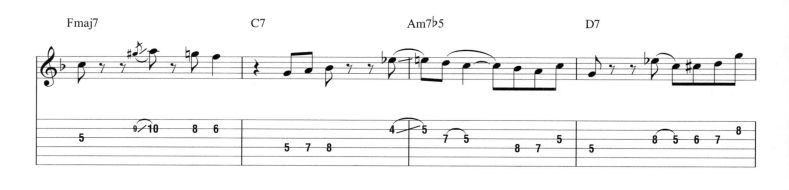

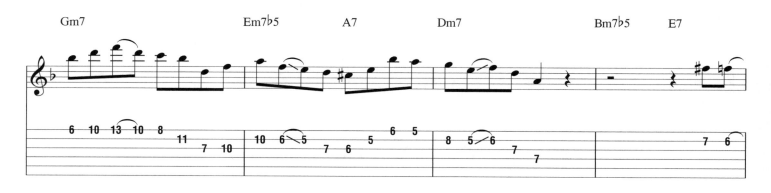

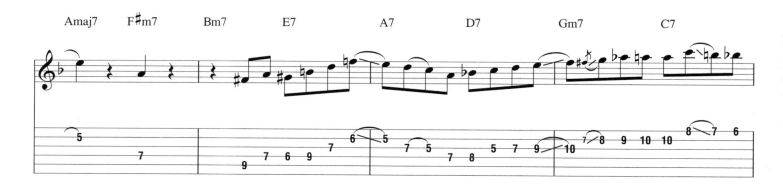

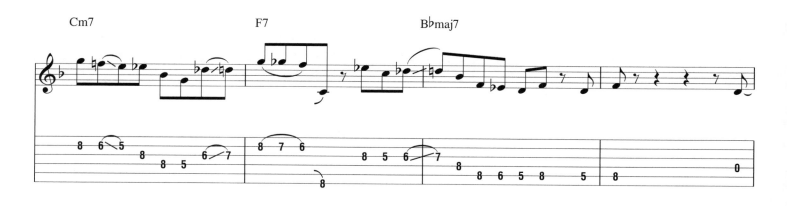

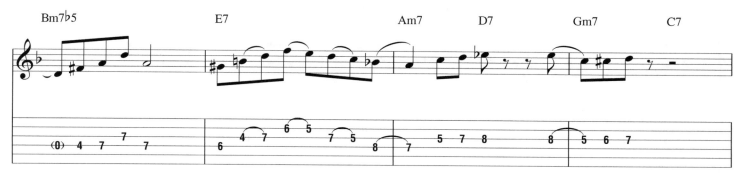

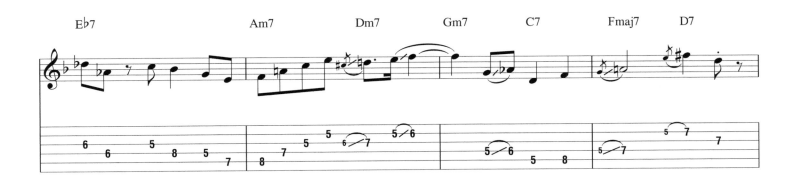

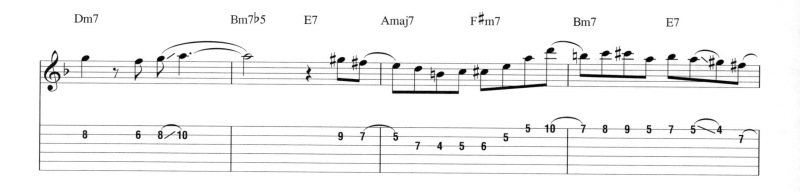

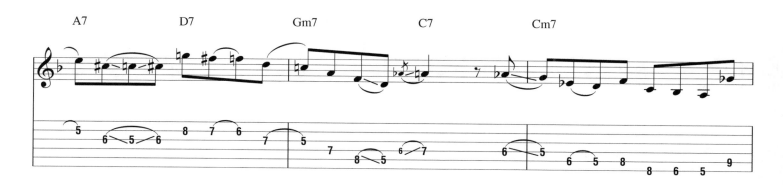

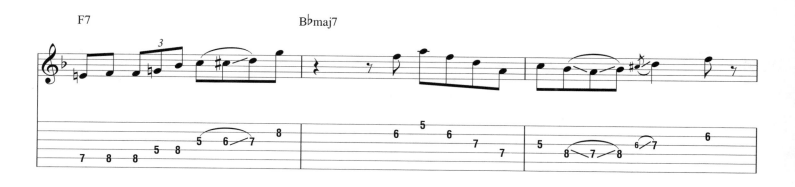

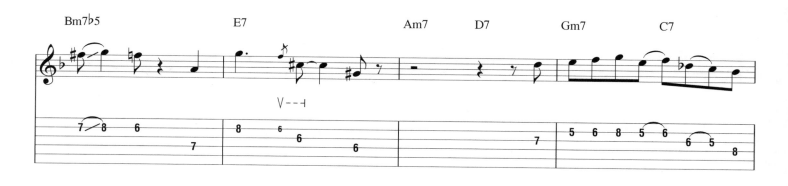

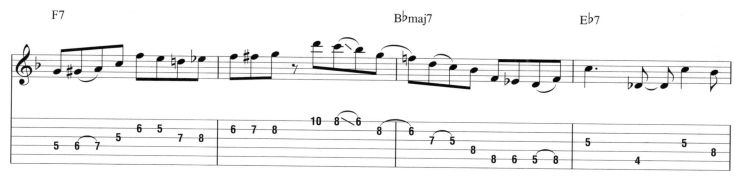

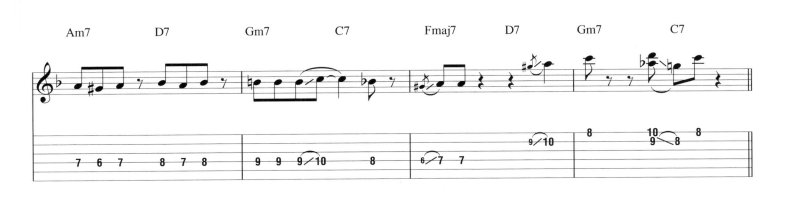

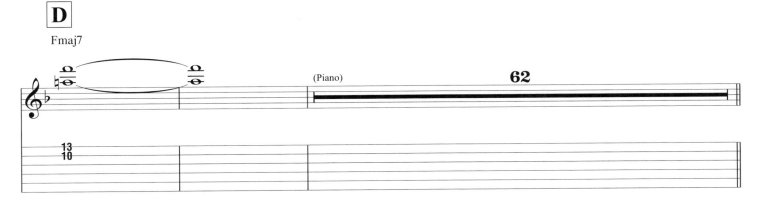

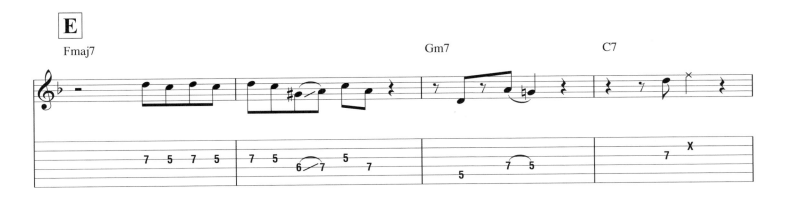

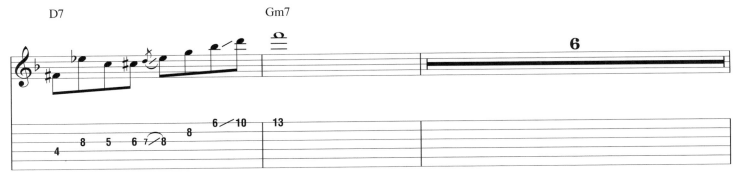

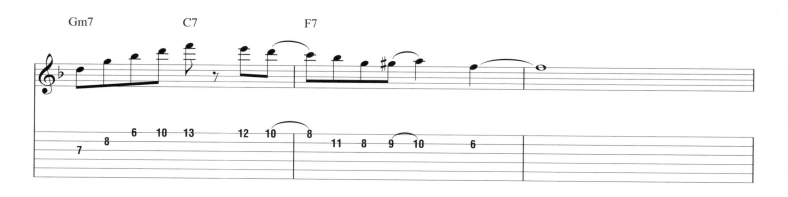

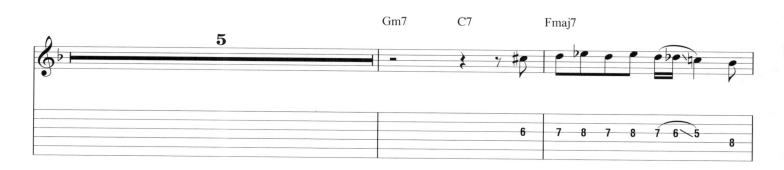

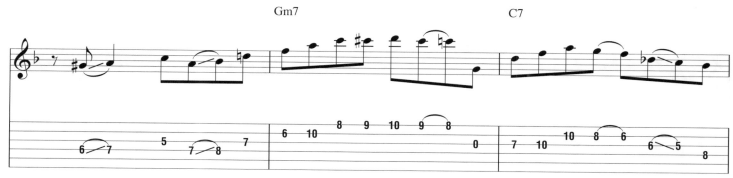

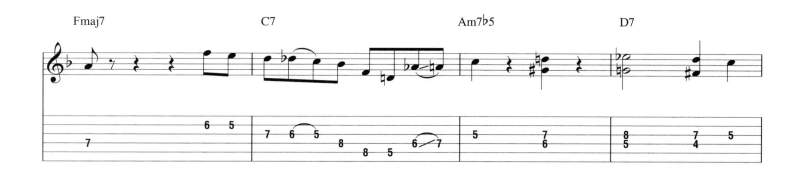

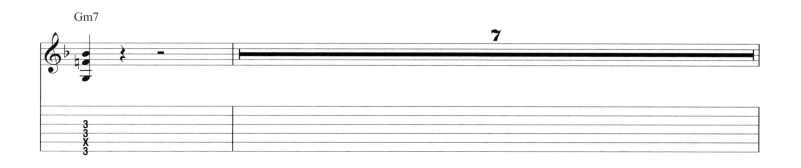

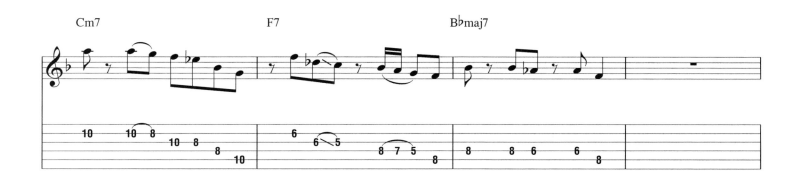

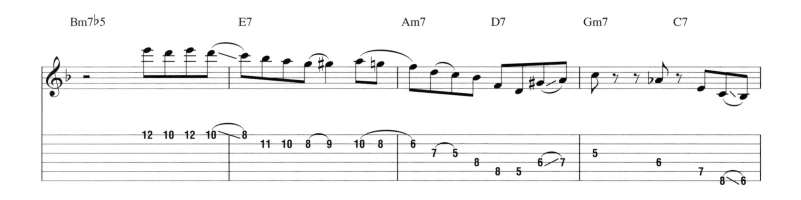

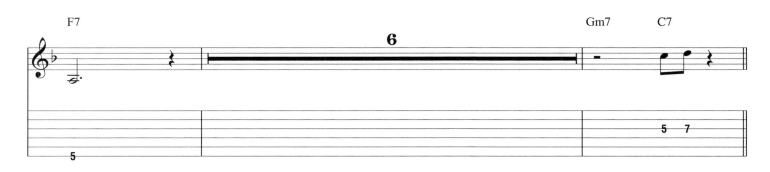

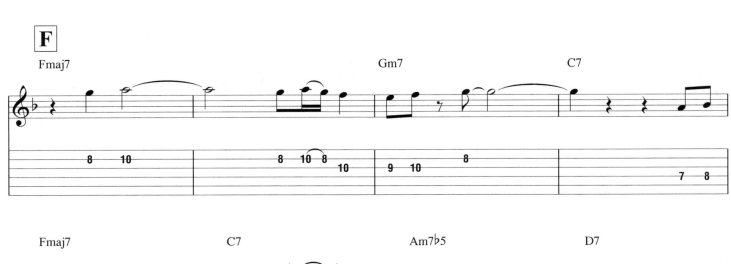

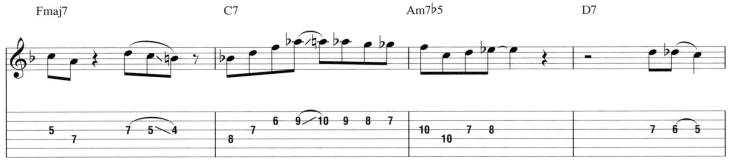

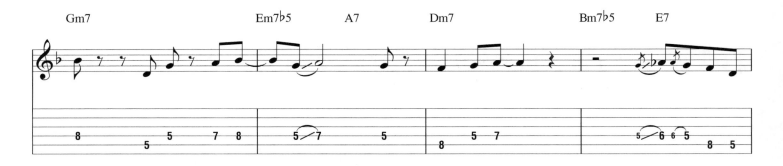

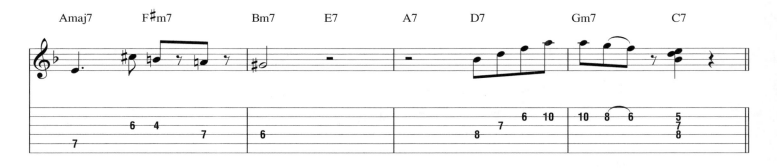

G

**Free time**

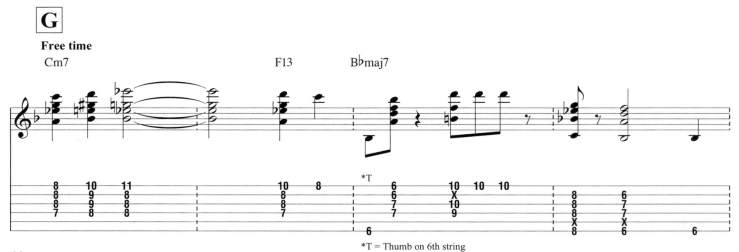

*T = Thumb on 6th string

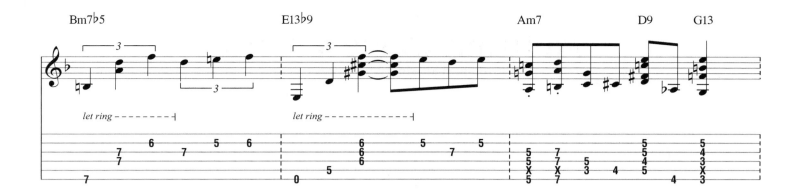

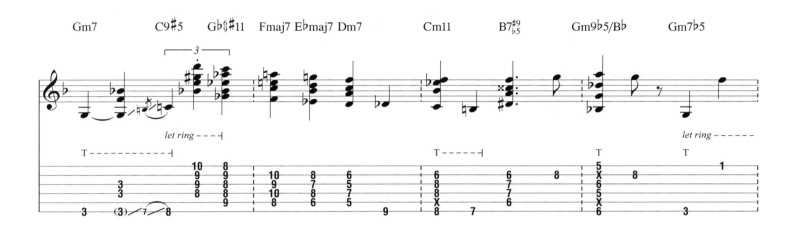

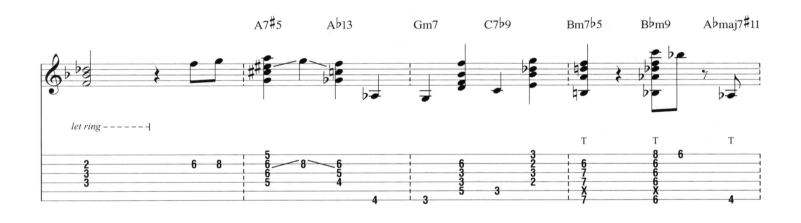

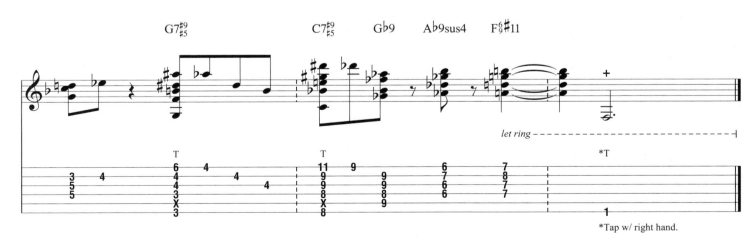

*Tap w/ right hand.

# Autumn in New York

## Words and Music by Vernon Duke

*Tuning:
(low to high) E-A♭-D-G-B-E

**A**

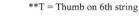

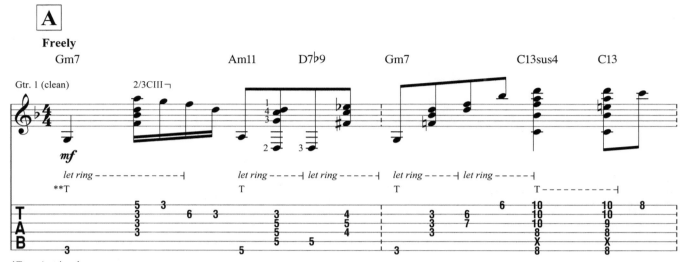

*Tune A string down one octave.
**T = Thumb on 6th string

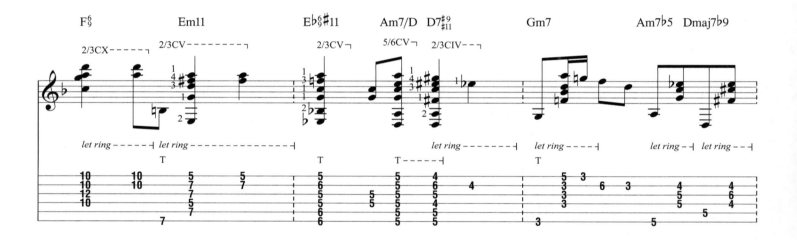

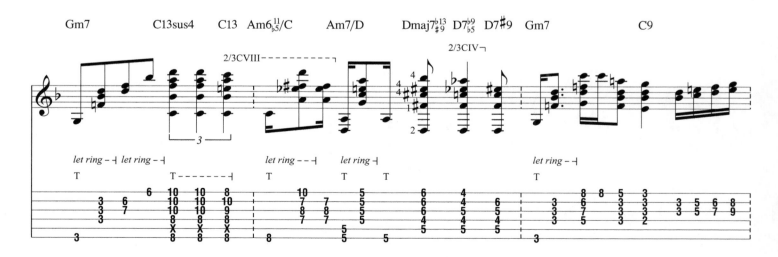

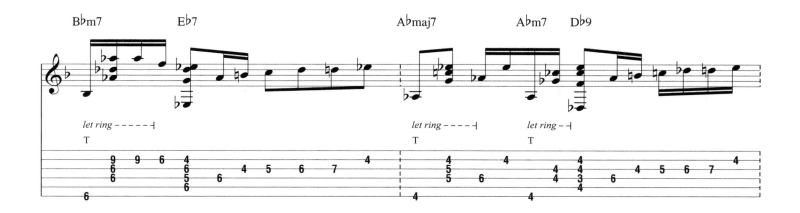

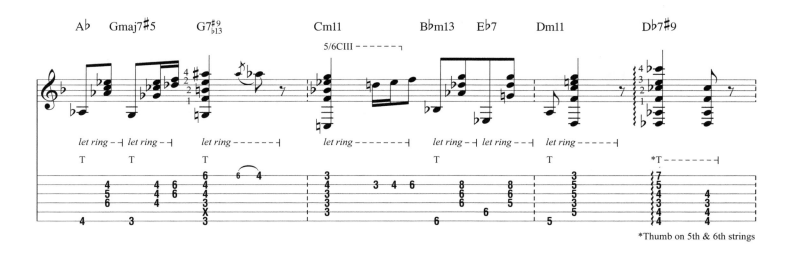

*Thumb on 5th & 6th strings

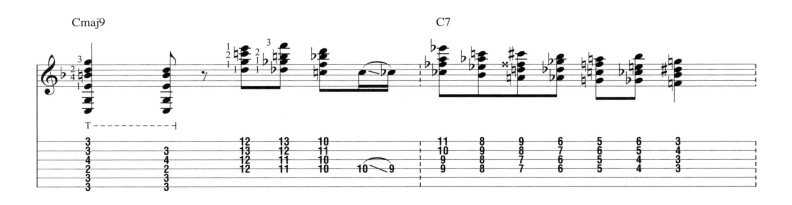

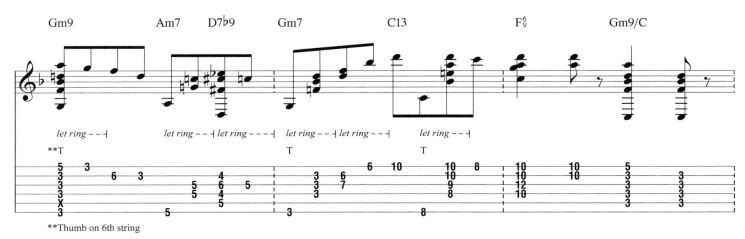

**Thumb on 6th string

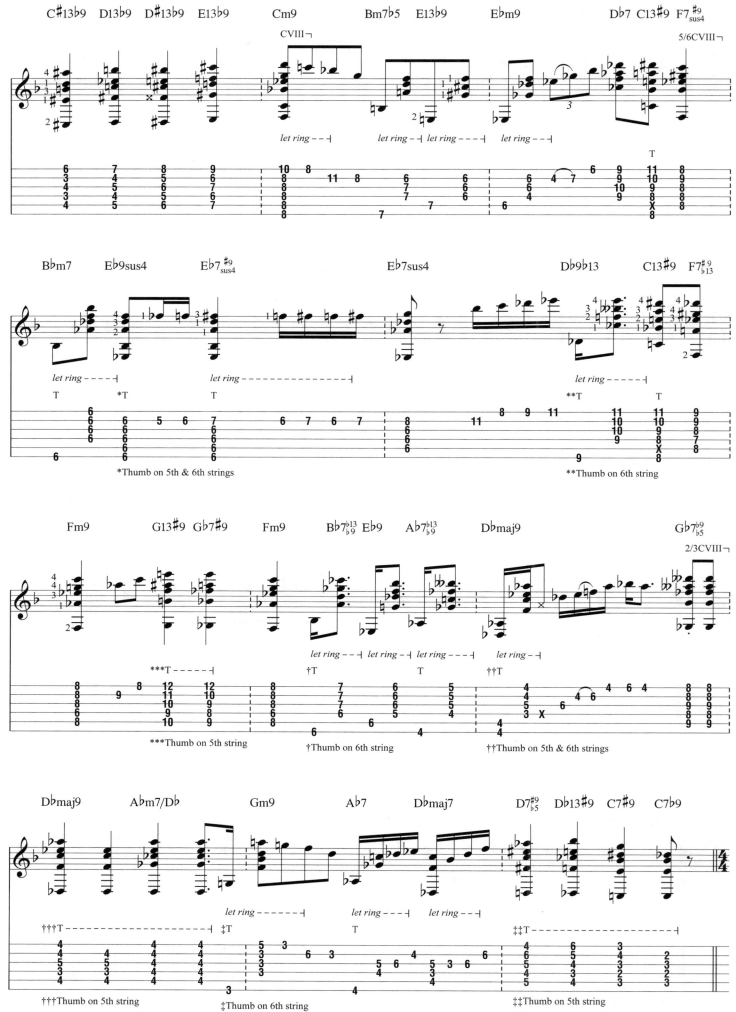

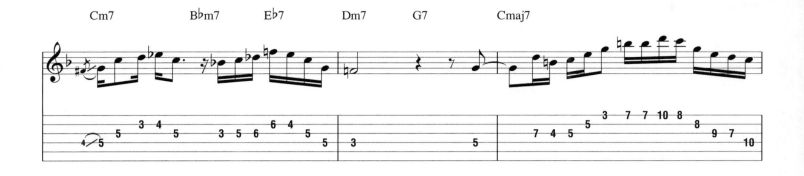

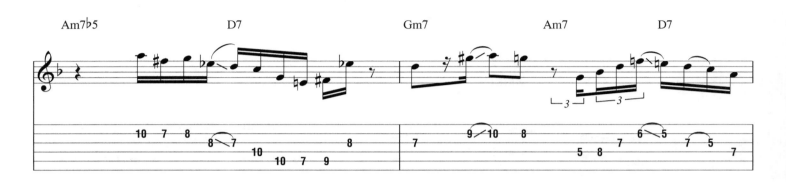

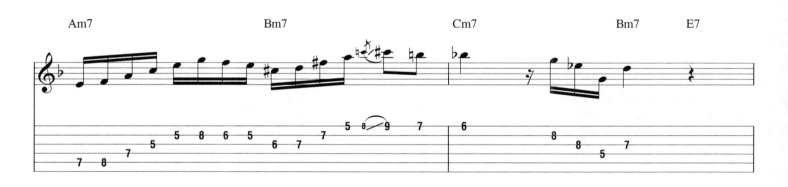

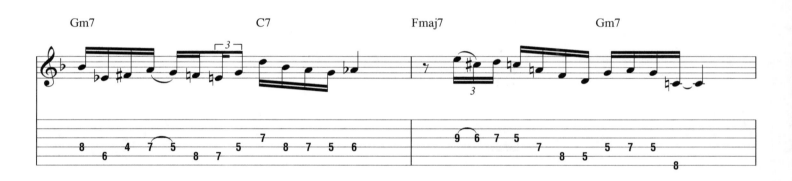

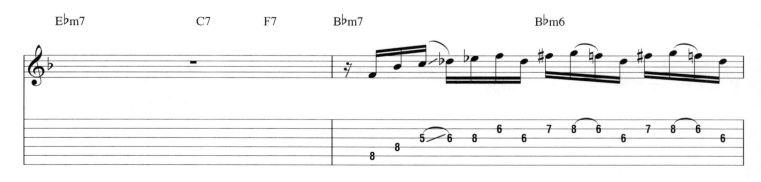

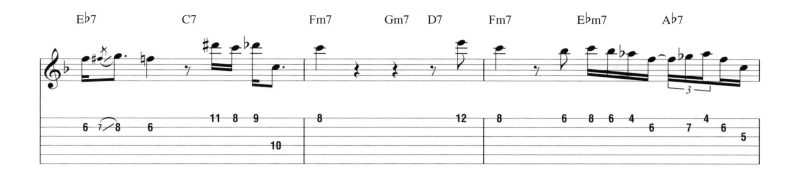

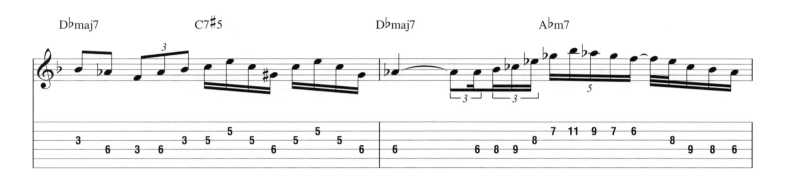

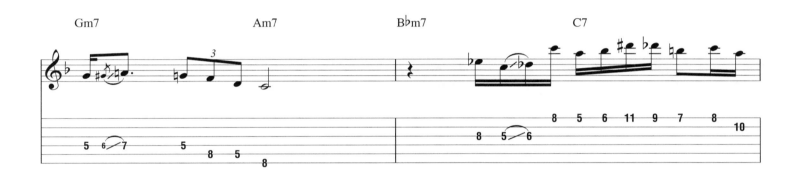

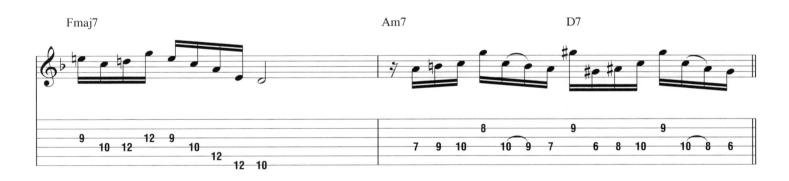

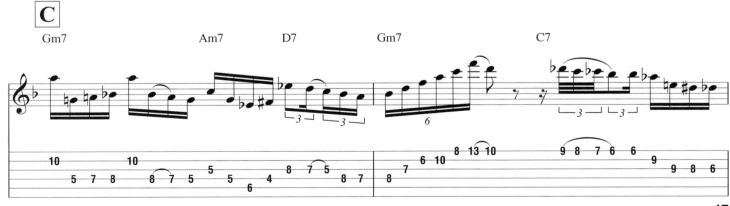

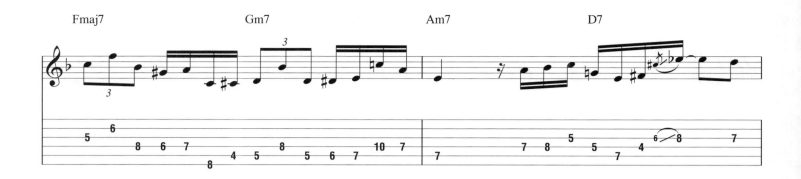

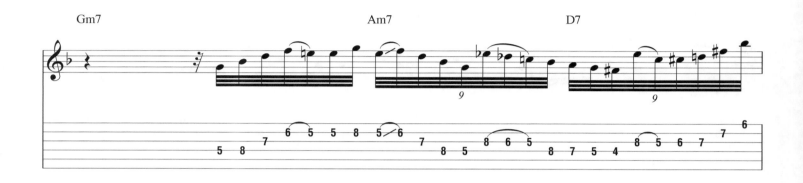

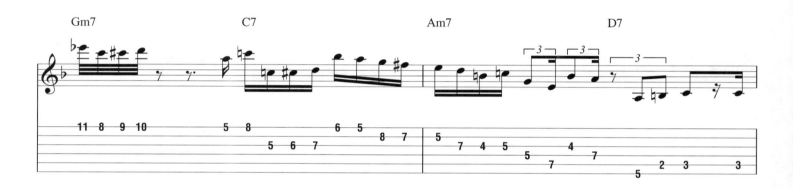

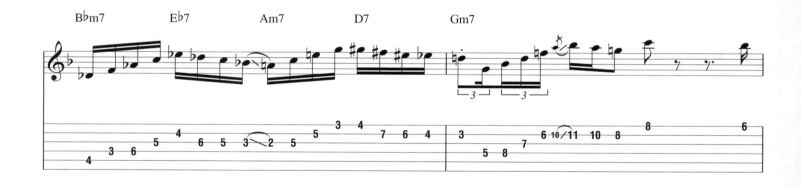

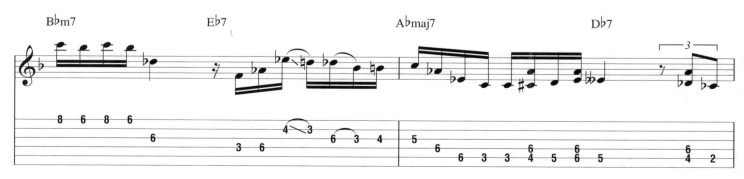

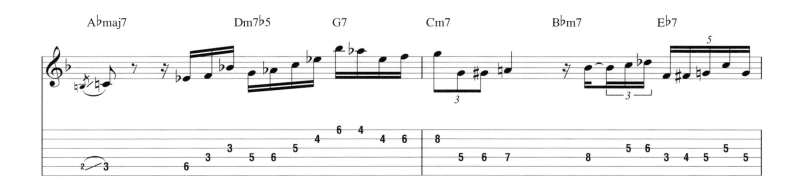

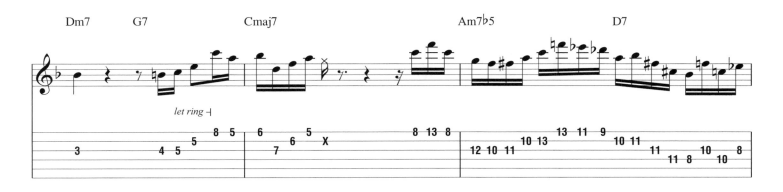

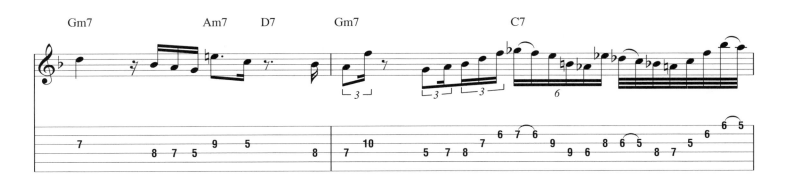

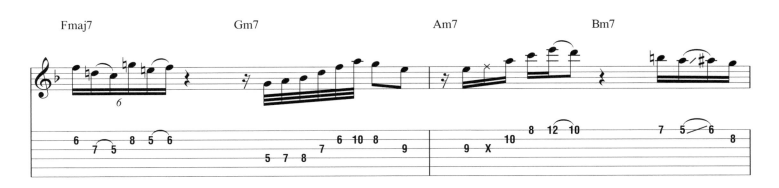

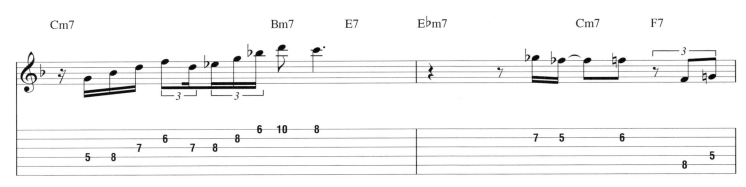

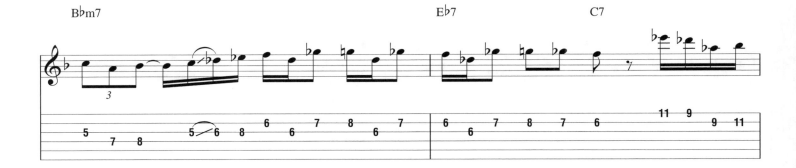

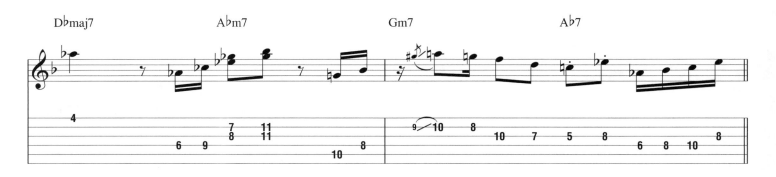

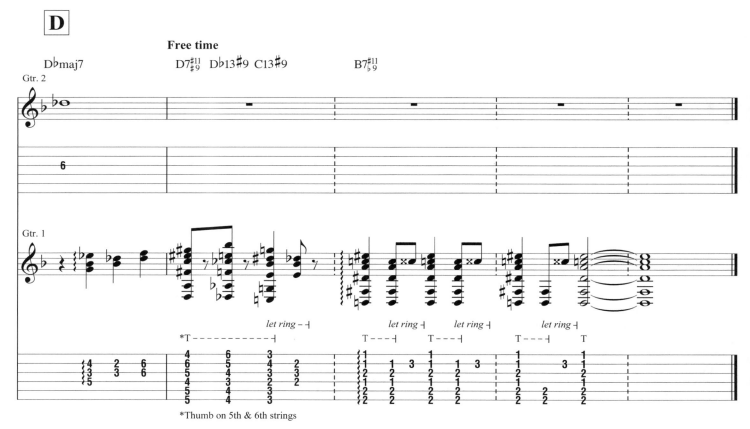

*Thumb on 5th & 6th strings

from *The Interpretations of Tal Farlow*

# Autumn Leaves

**English lyric by Johnny Mercer**
**French lyric by Jacques Prevert**
**Music by Joseph Kosma**

*Tuning:
(low to high) E-A↓-D-G-B-E

**A**

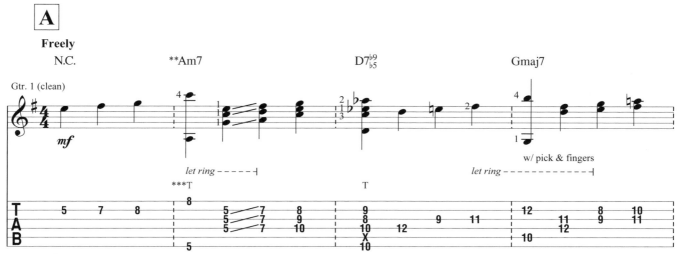

*Tune A string down one octave.     **Chord symbols reflect implied harmony.
***T = Thumb on 6th string

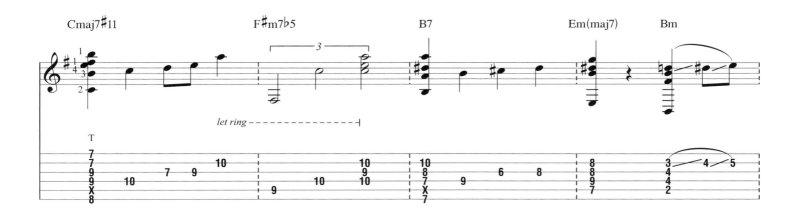

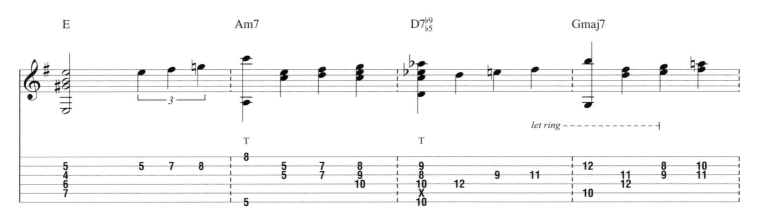

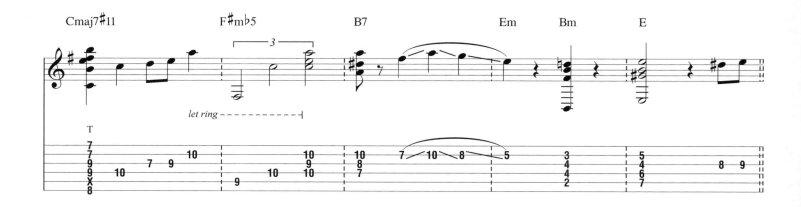

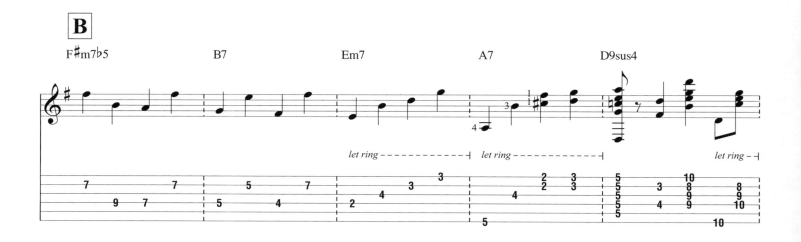

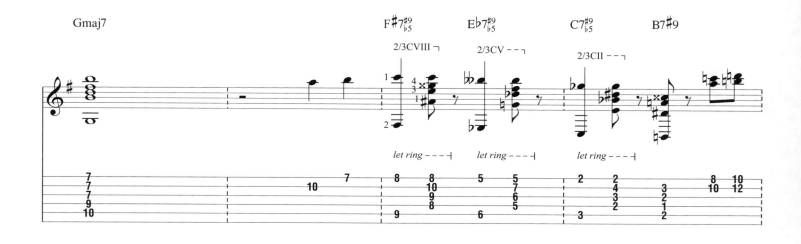

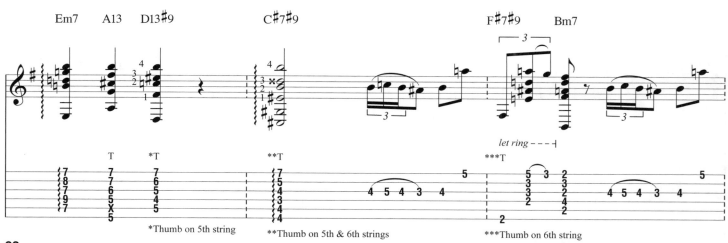

*Thumb on 5th string          **Thumb on 5th & 6th strings          ***Thumb on 6th string

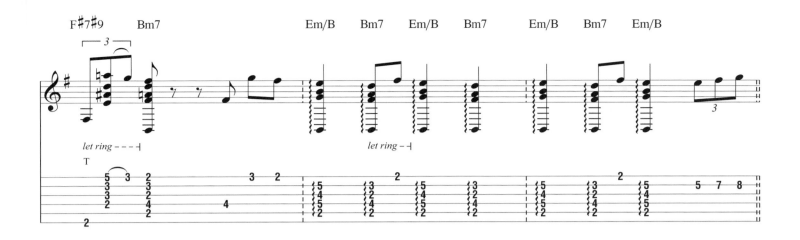

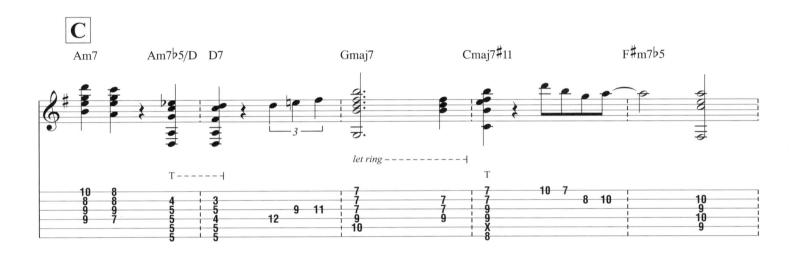

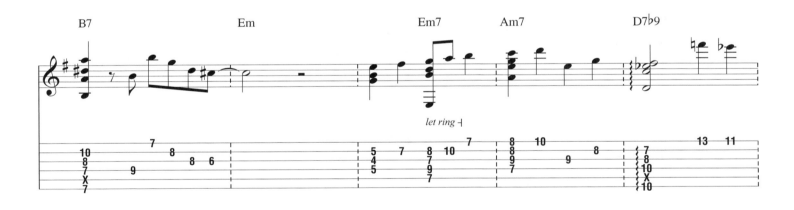

**D**

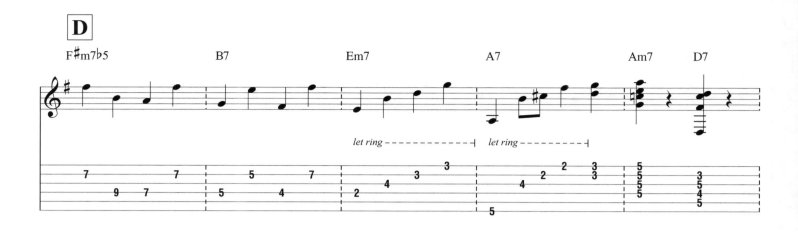

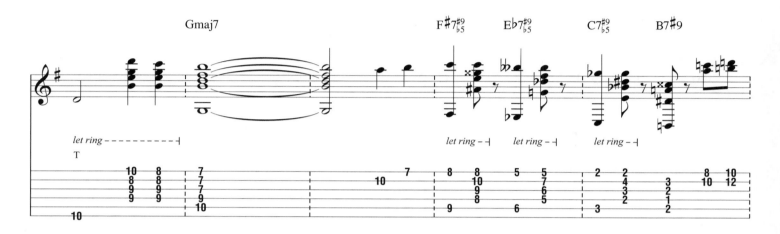

*Thumb on 5th & 6th strings

**Thumb on 6th string

***Thumb on 5th string

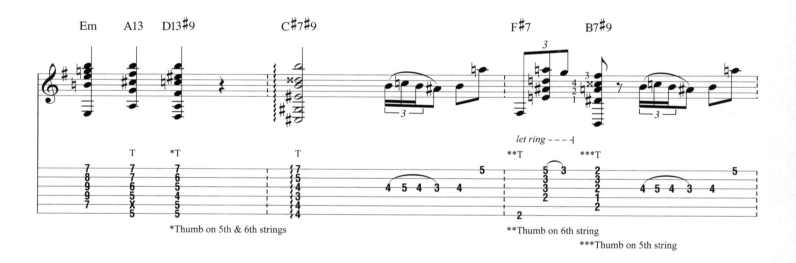

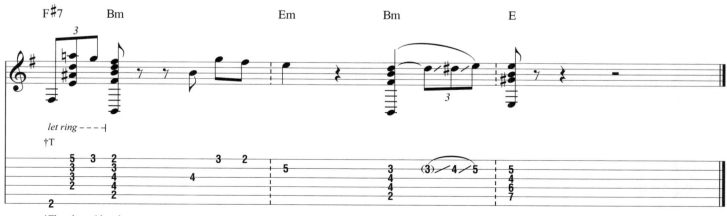

†Thumb on 6th string

from *Chromatic Palette*

# Blue Art, Too

### By Tal Farlow

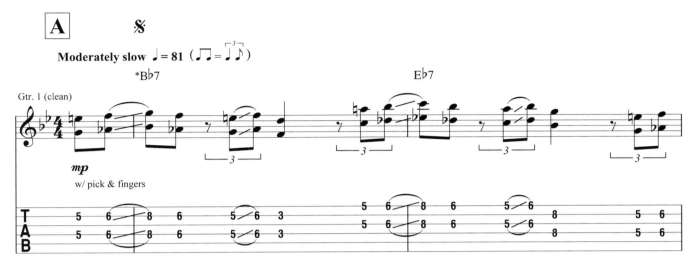

*Chord symbols reflect overall harmony.

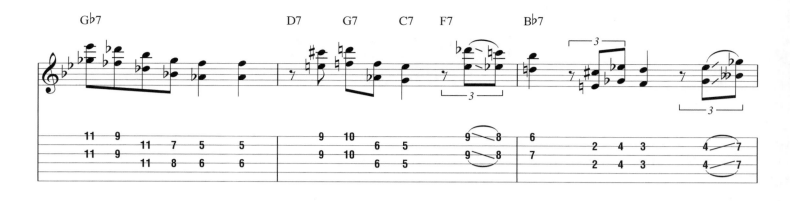

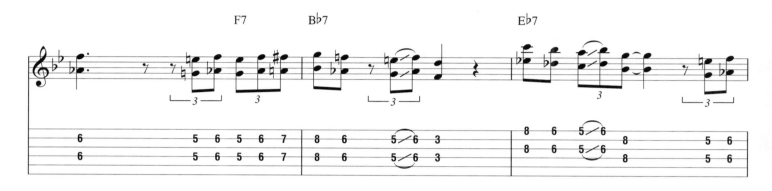

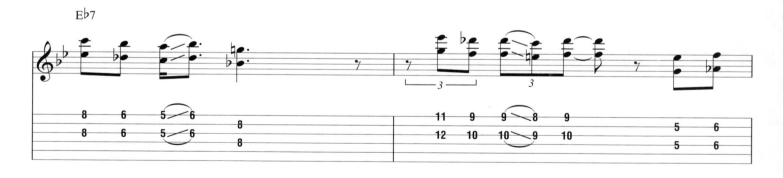

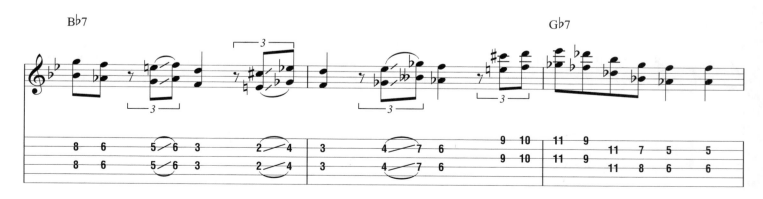

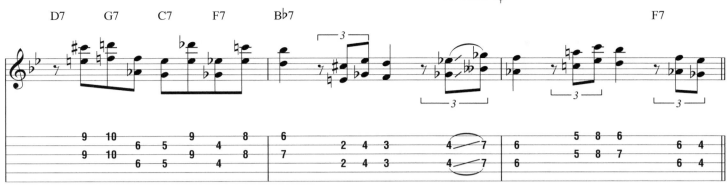

## B

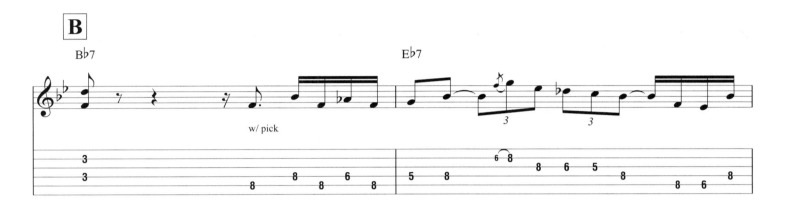

*Played as even eighth notes.

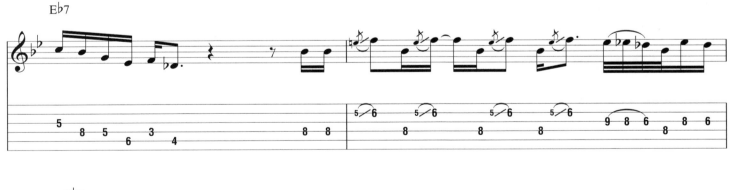

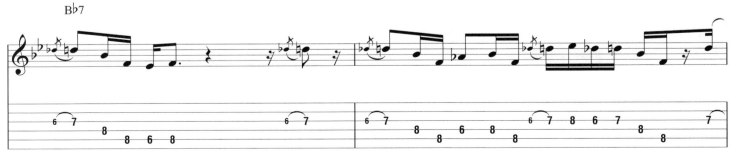

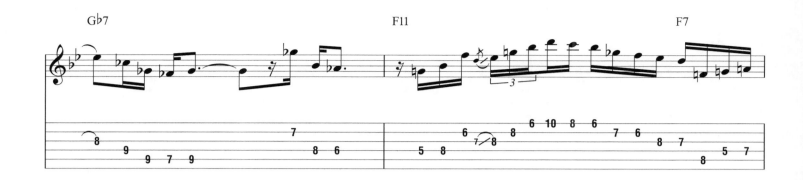

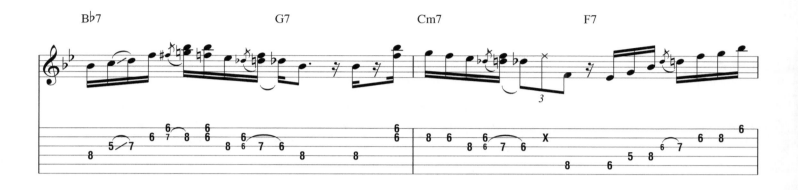

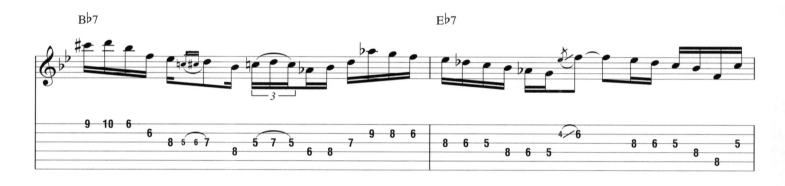

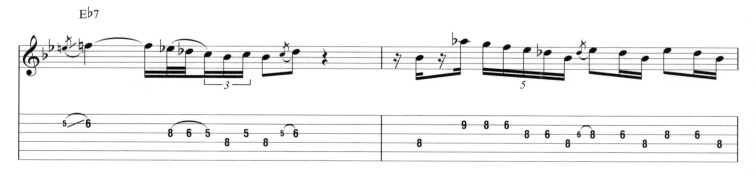

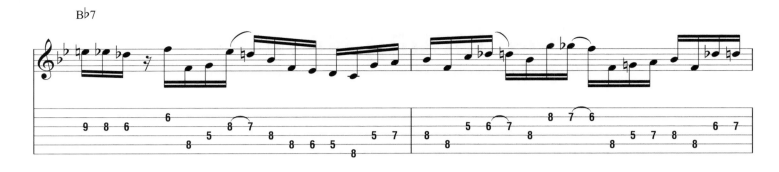

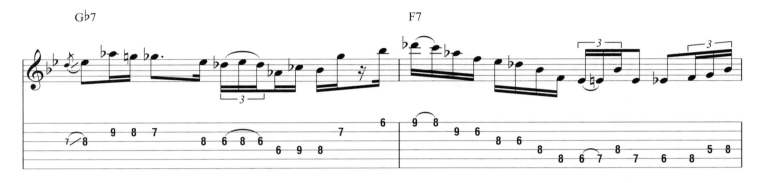

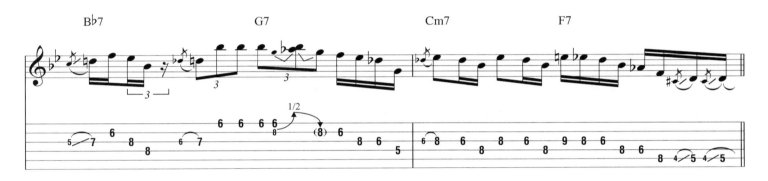

**C**

**⊕ Coda**

**D.S. al Coda**

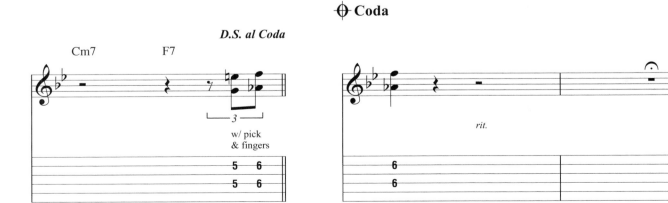

from *A Sign of the Times*

# Fascinating Rhythm

### Music and Lyrics by George Gershwin and Ira Gershwin

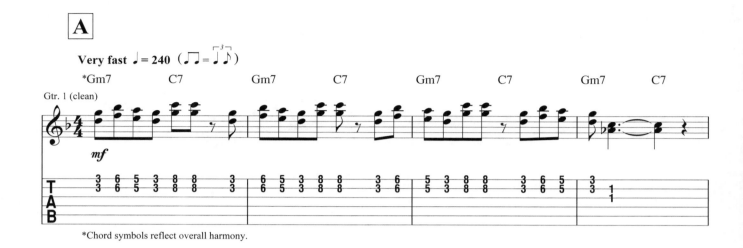

*Chord symbols reflect overall harmony.

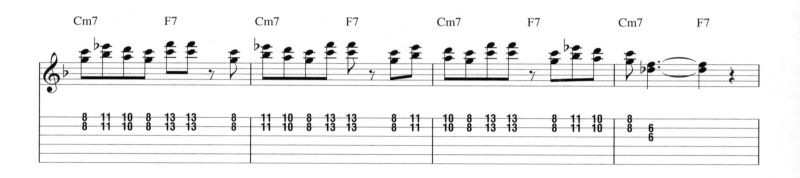

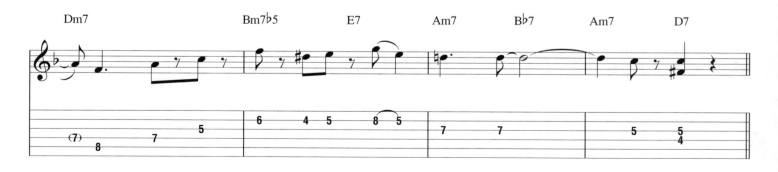

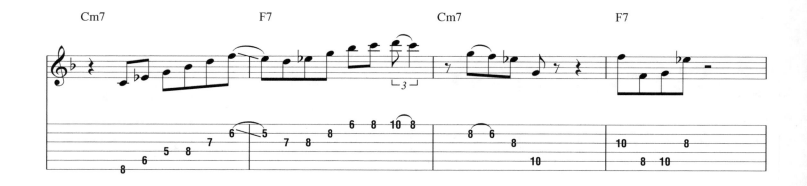

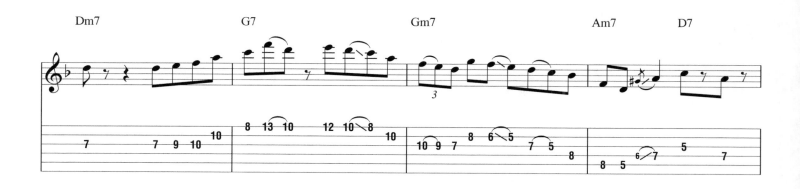

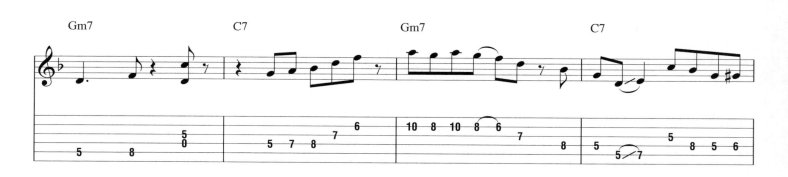

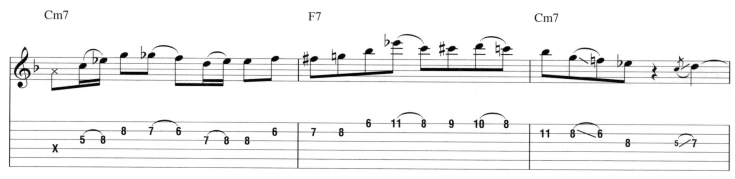

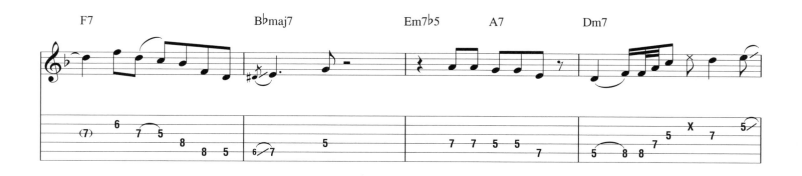

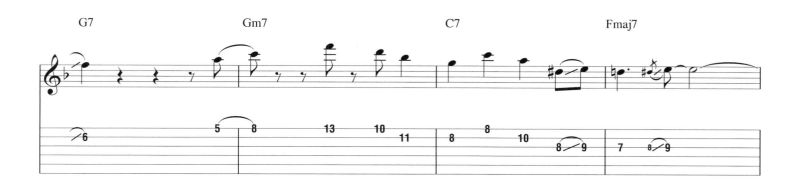

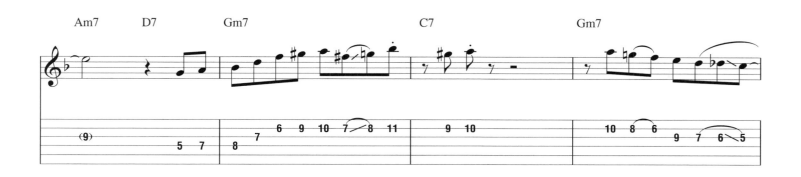

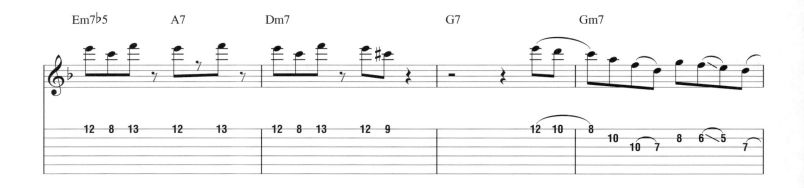

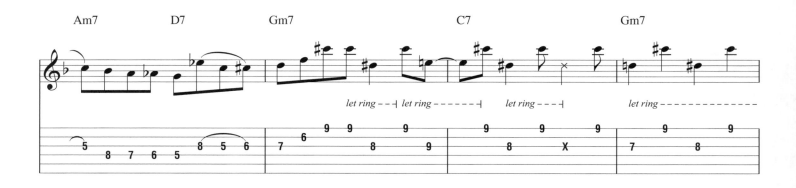

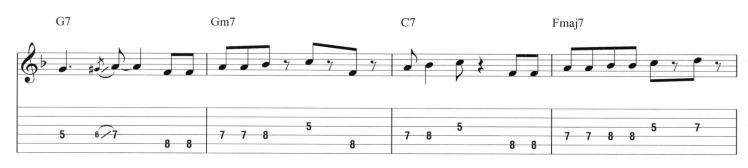

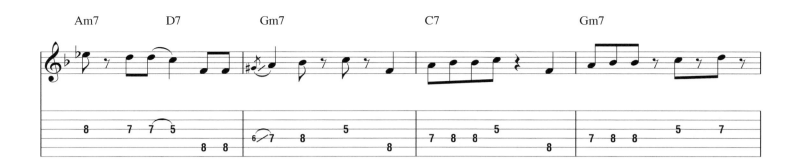

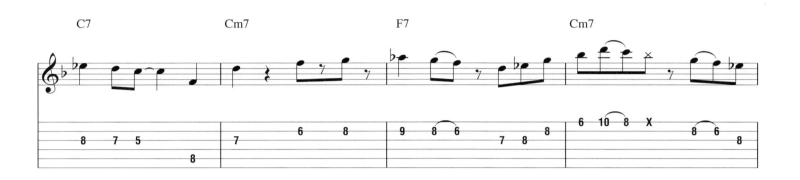

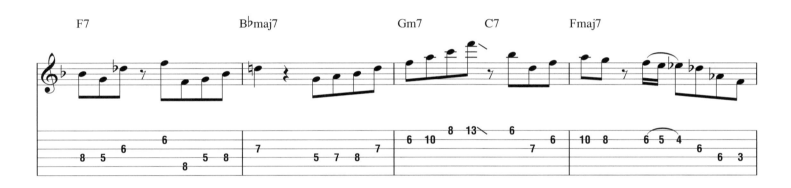

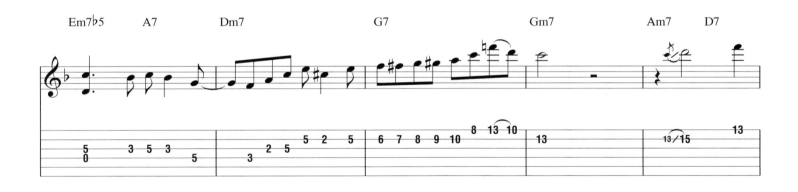

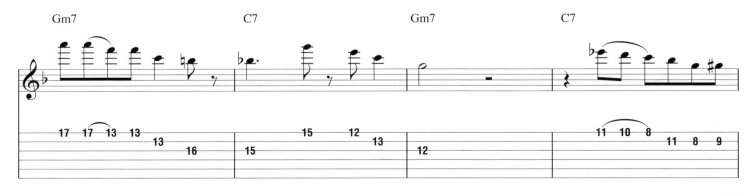

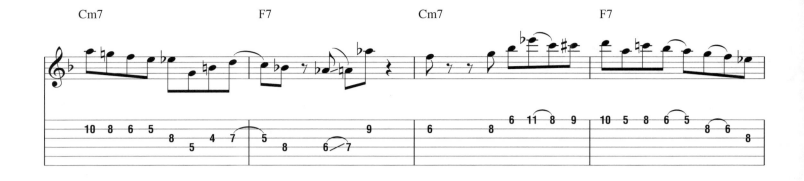

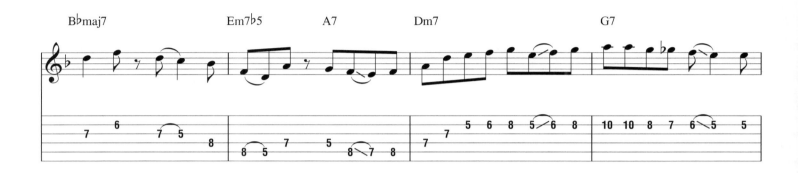

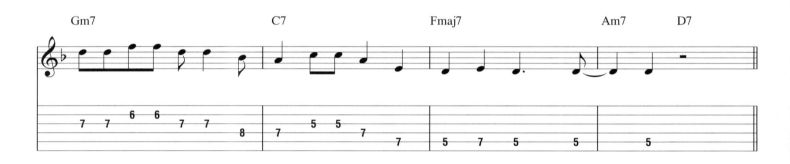

**E**

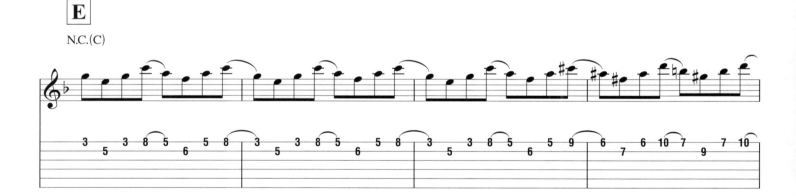

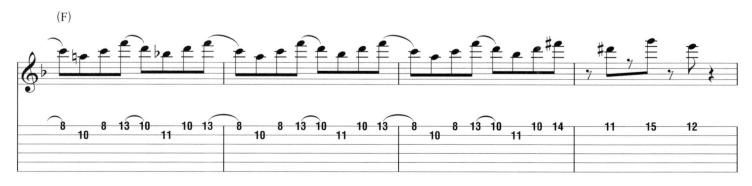

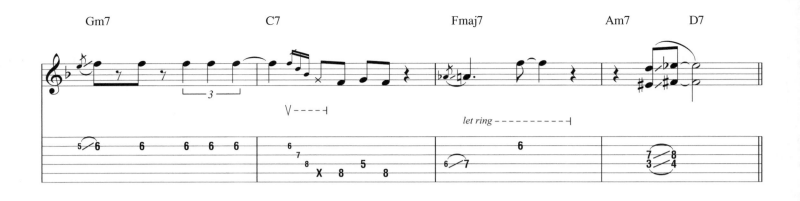

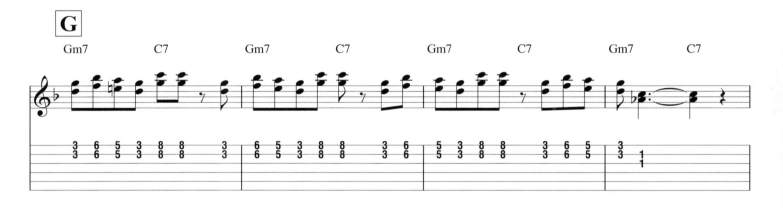

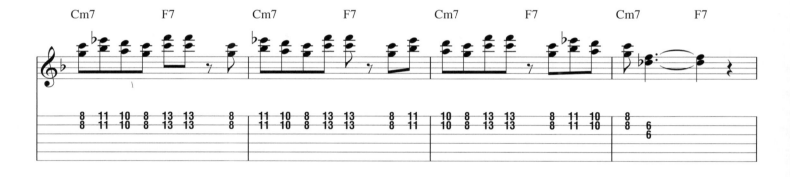

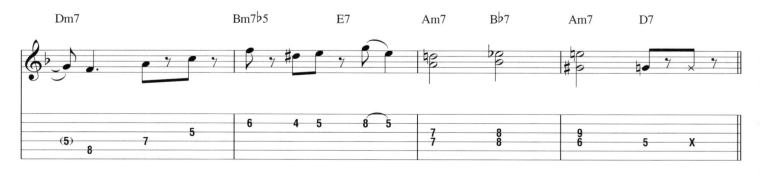

from *Tal Farlow '78*

# Mahoney's 11 Ohms

## By Tal Farlow

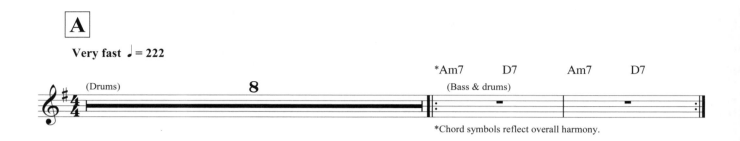

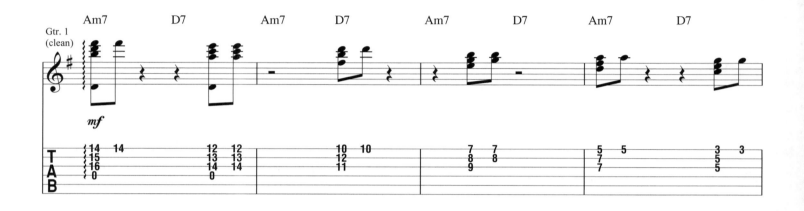

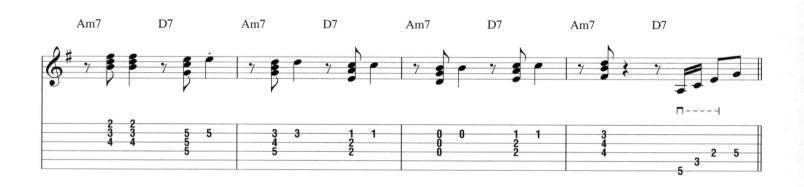

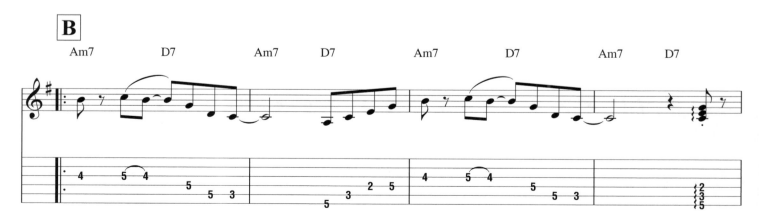

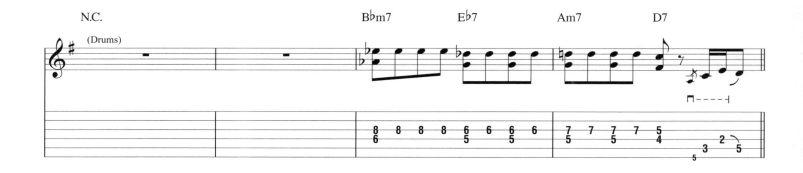

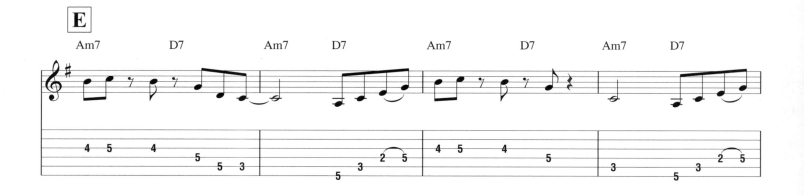

**E**

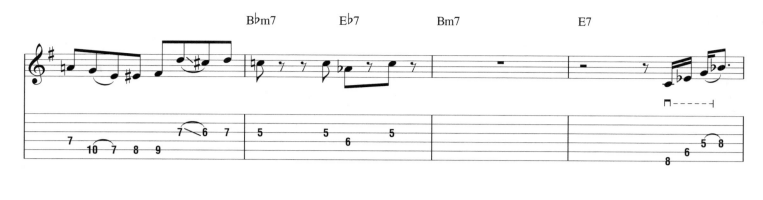

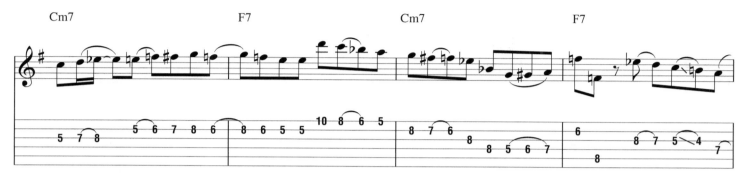

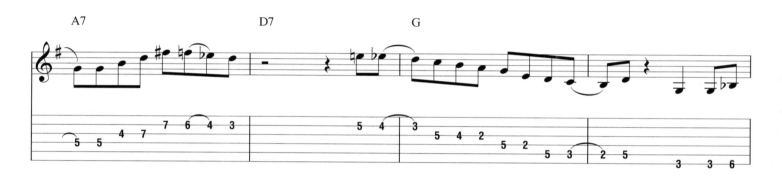

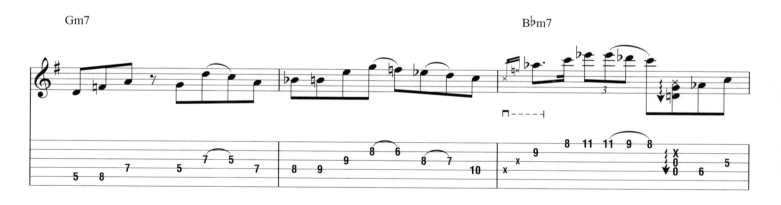

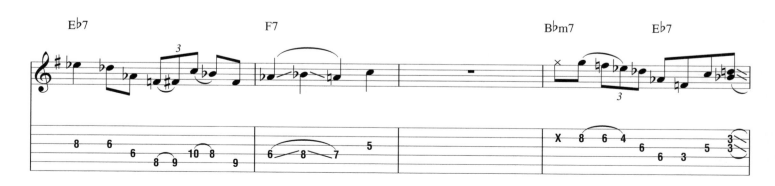

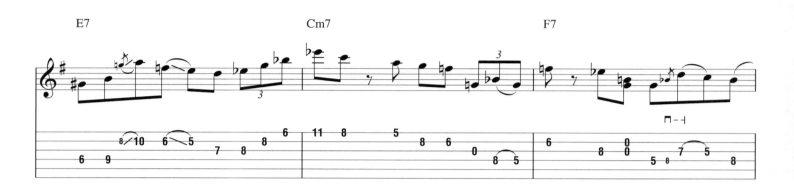

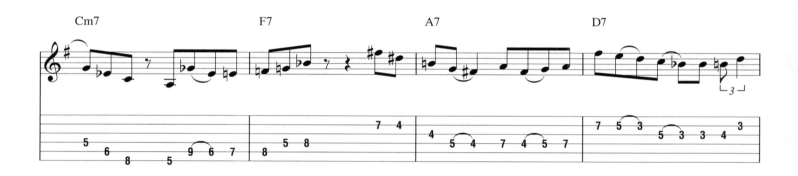

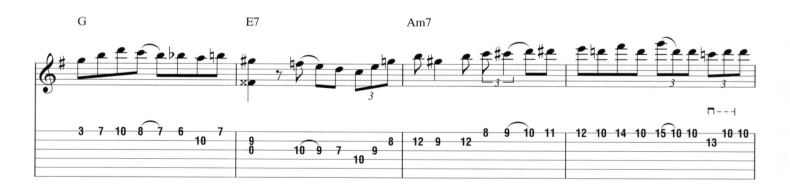

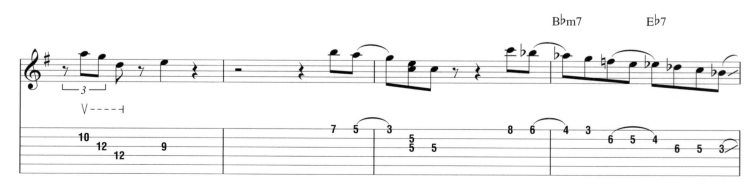

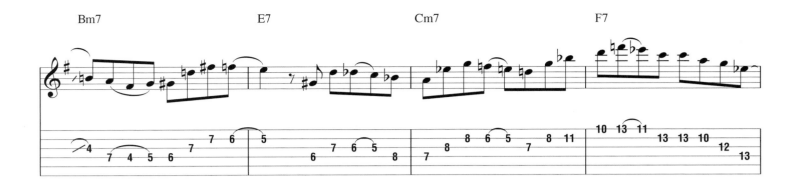

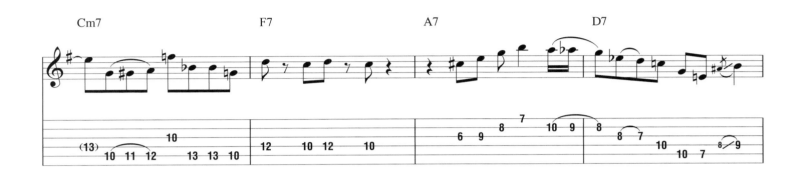

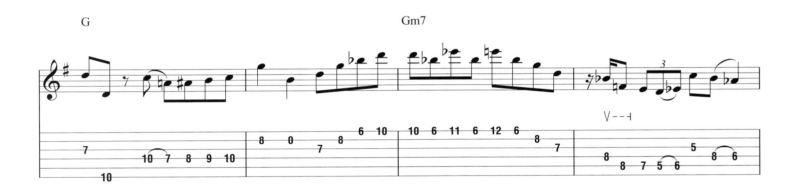

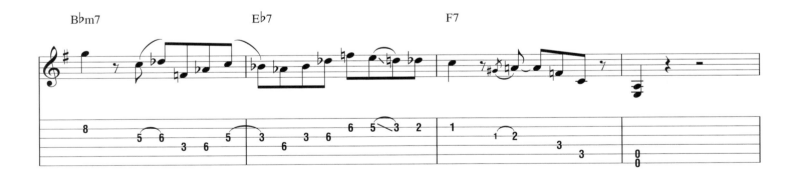

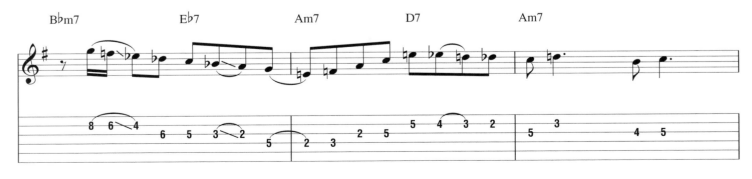

Bbm7    Eb7    Bm7    E7    Cm7

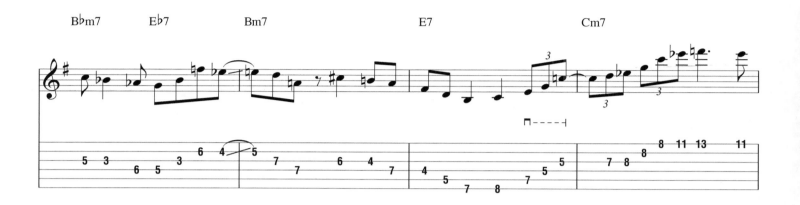

F7    Bm7    E7    A7

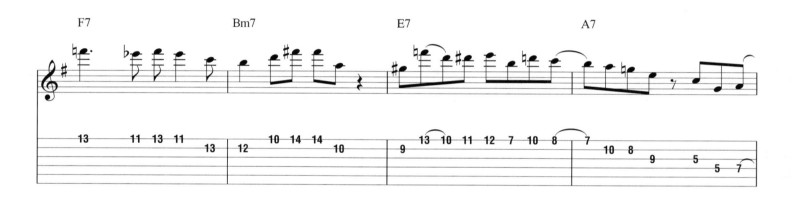

D7    G    E7    Am7

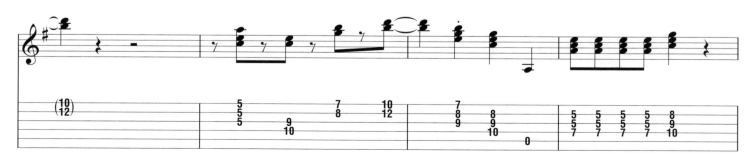

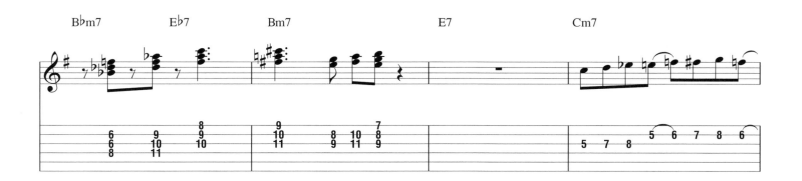

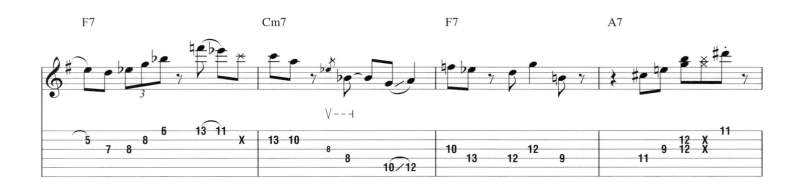

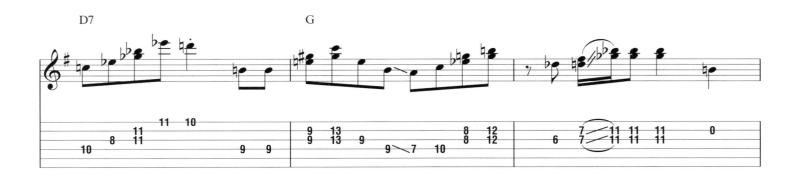

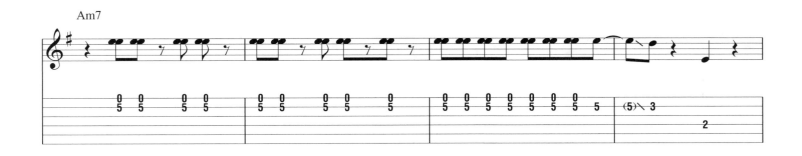

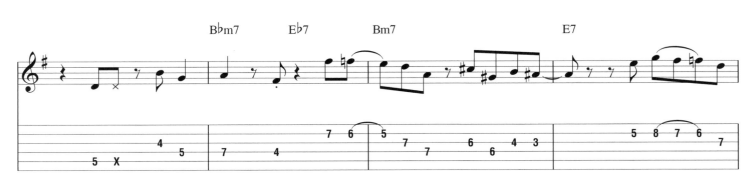

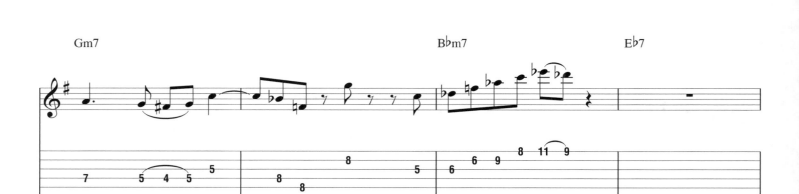

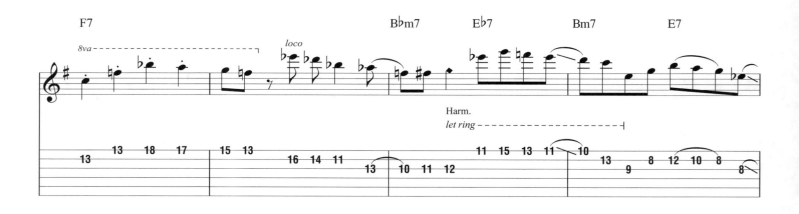

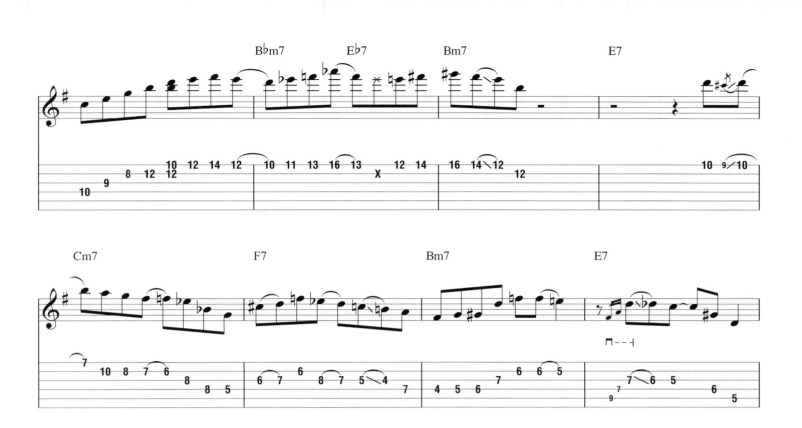

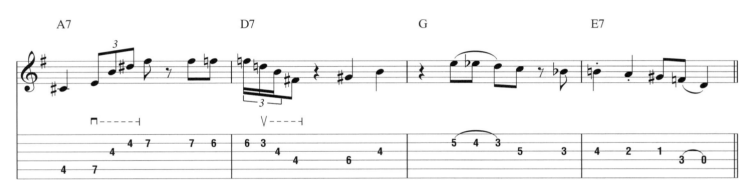

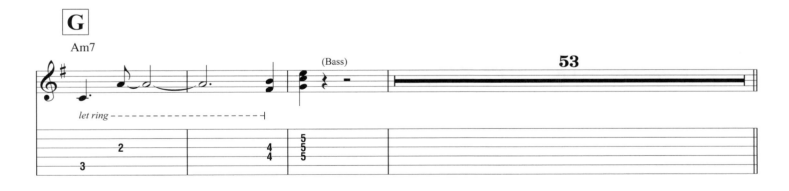

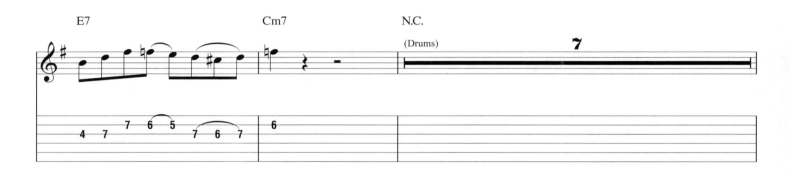

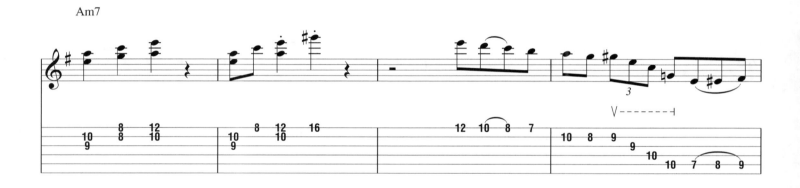

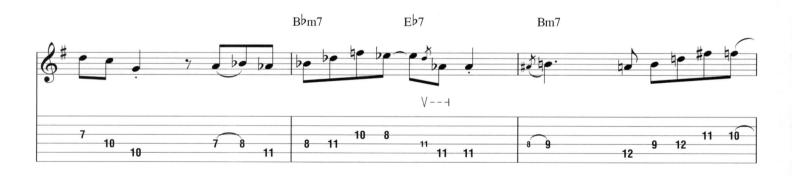

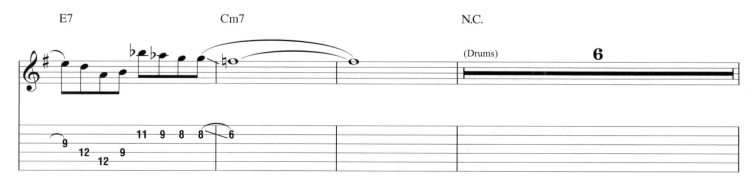

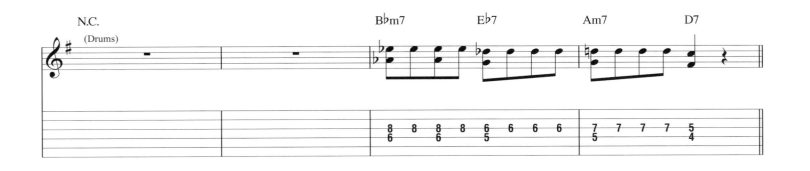

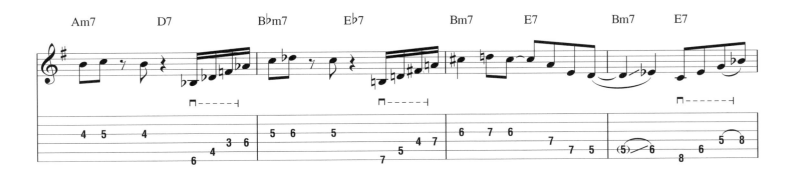

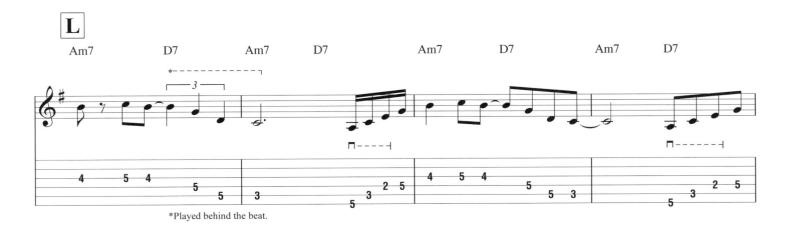

# Night and Day

**Words and Music by Cole Porter**

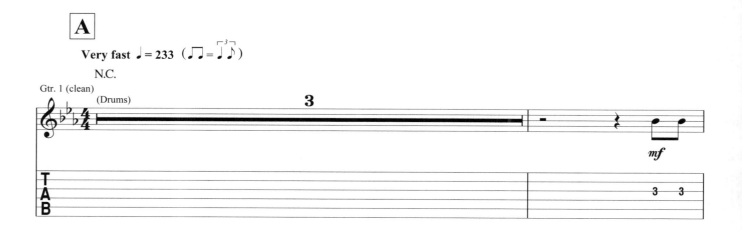

*Chord symbols reflect overall harmony.

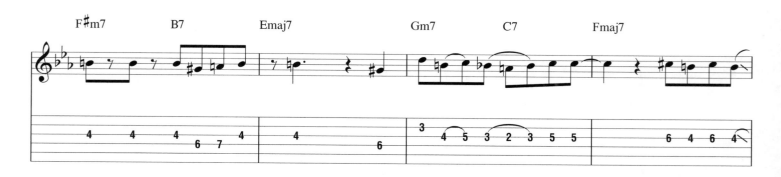

## B

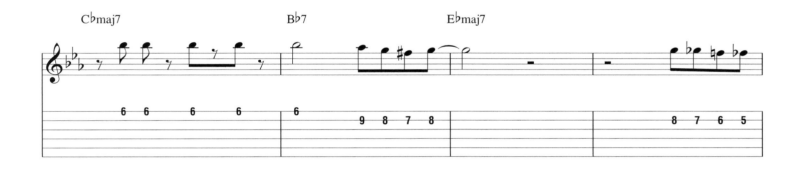

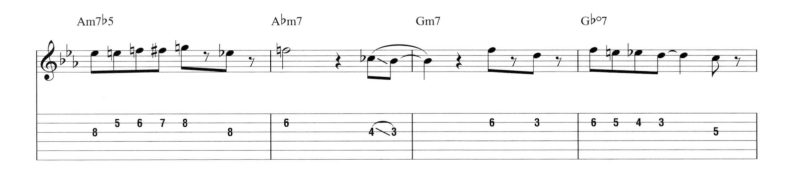

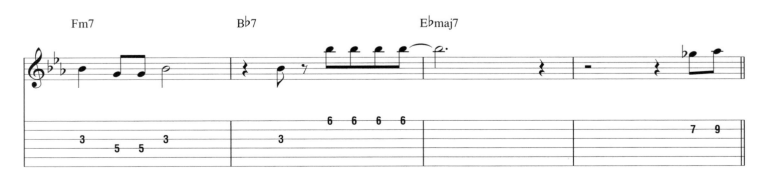

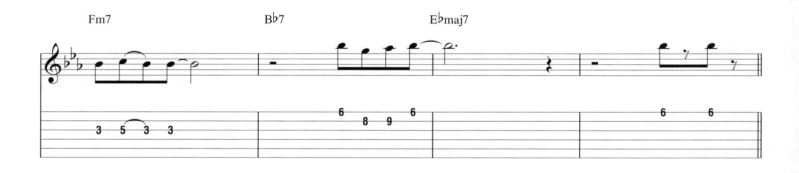

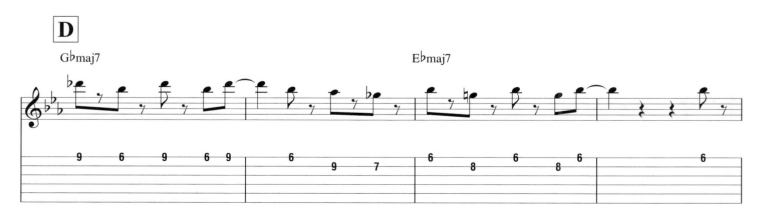

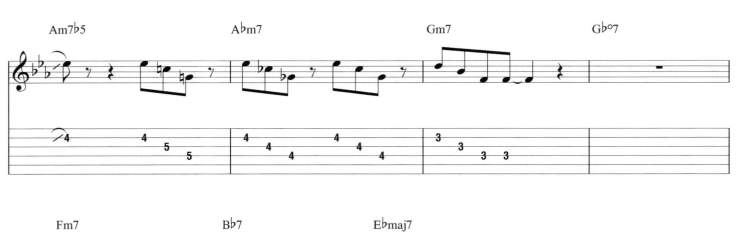

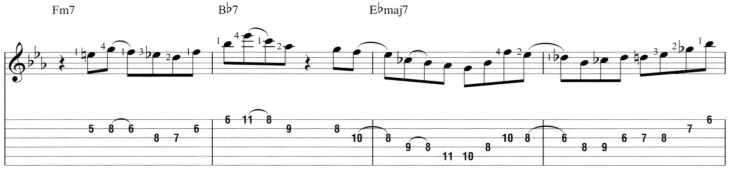

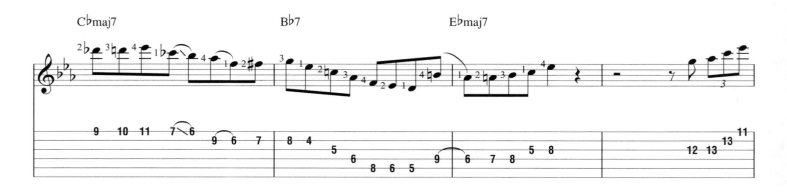

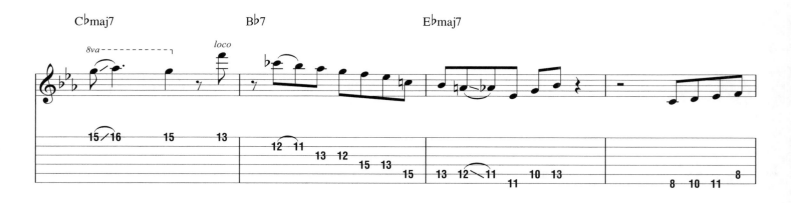

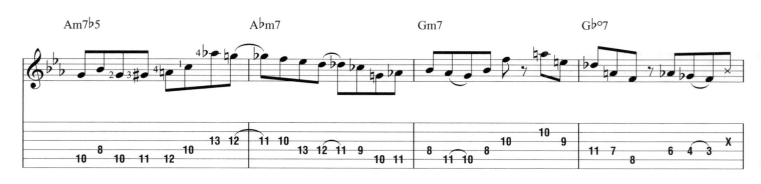

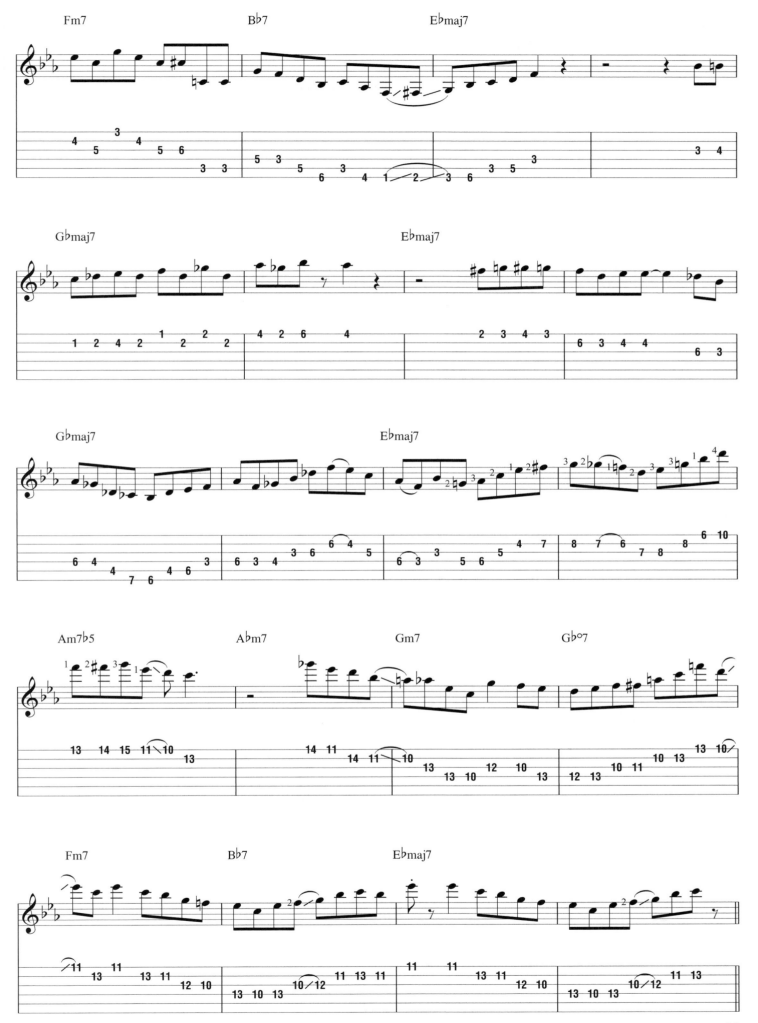

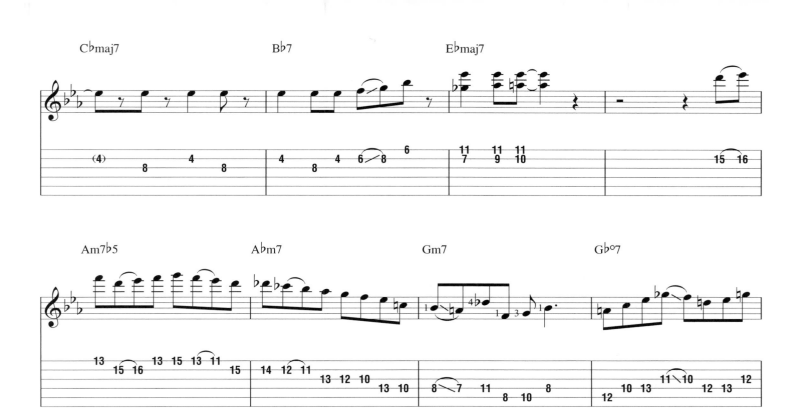

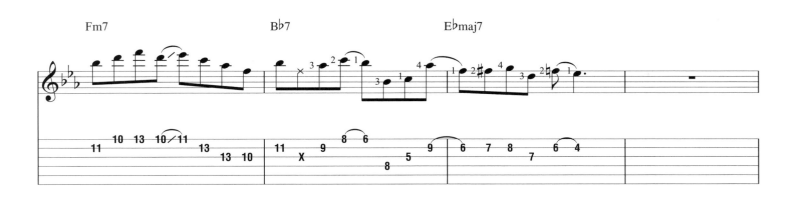

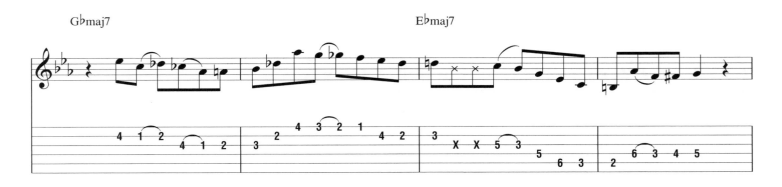

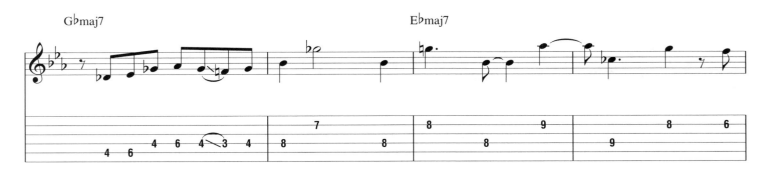

## I

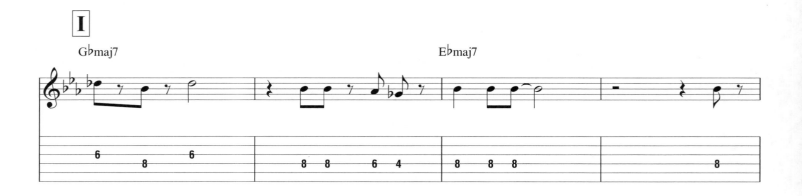

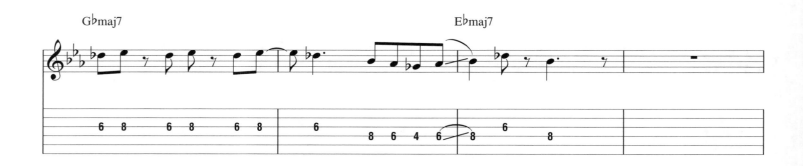

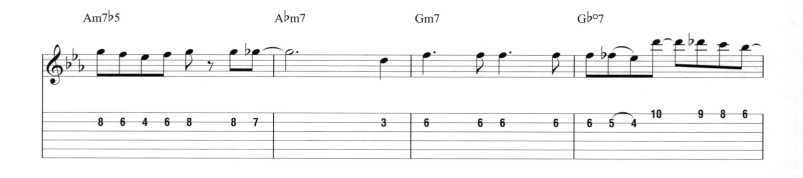

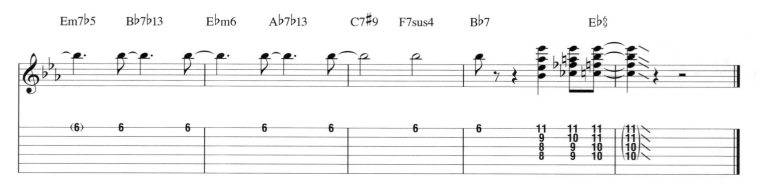

from *This Is Tal Farlow*

# Stella by Starlight

from the Paramount Picture THE UNINVITED
### Words by Ned Washington
### Music by Victor Young

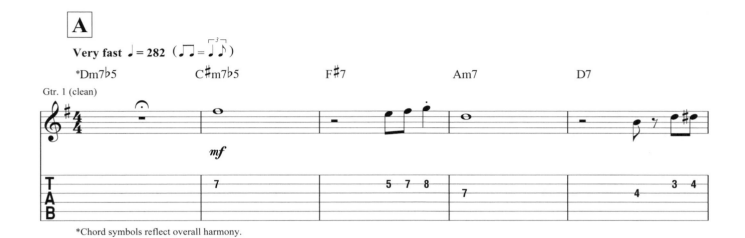

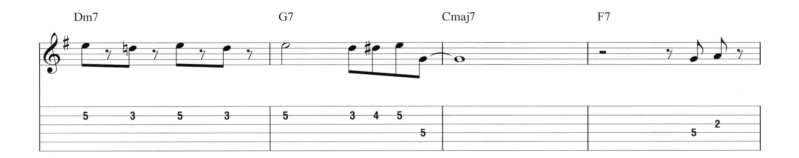

**B**

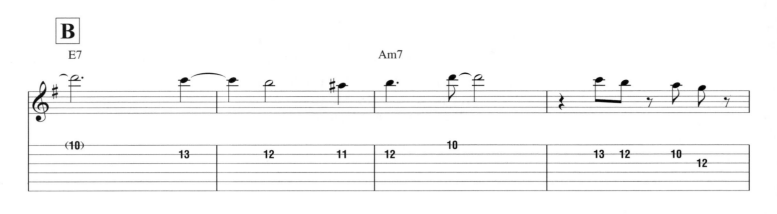

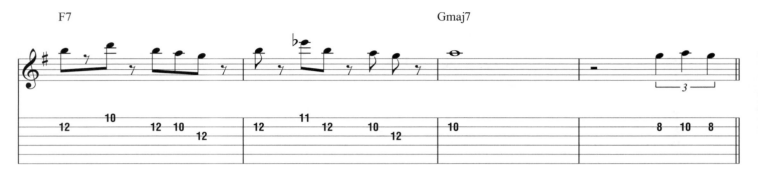

**C**

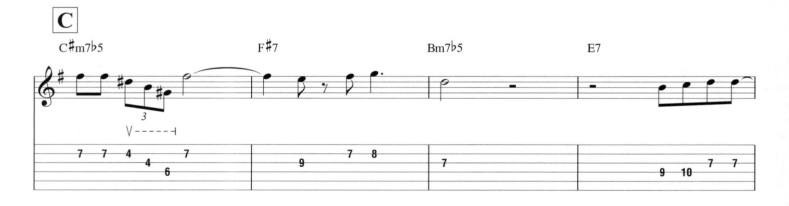

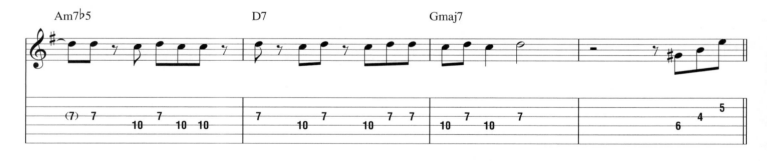

**D**

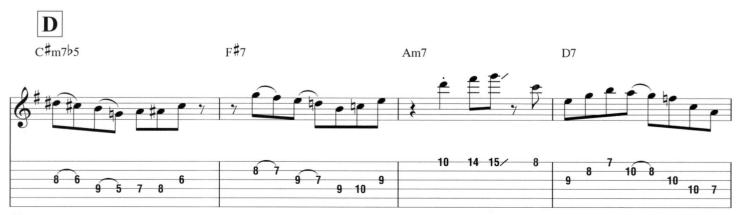

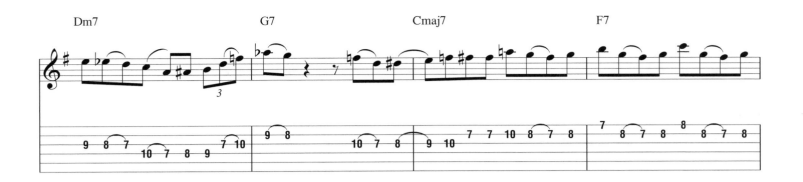

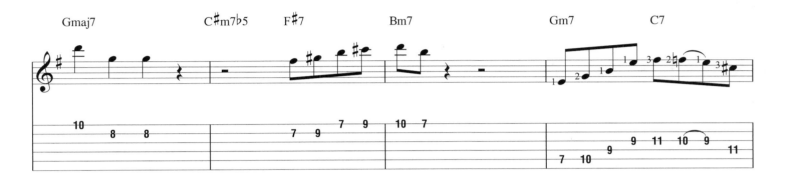

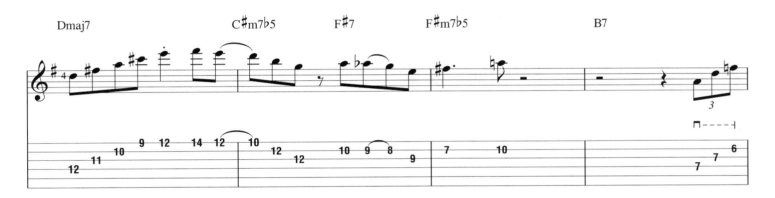

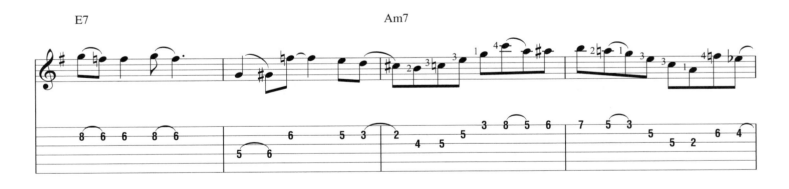

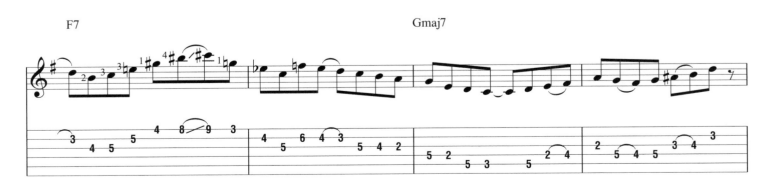

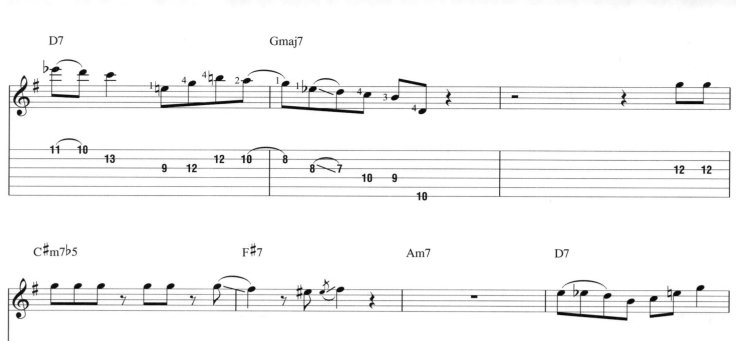

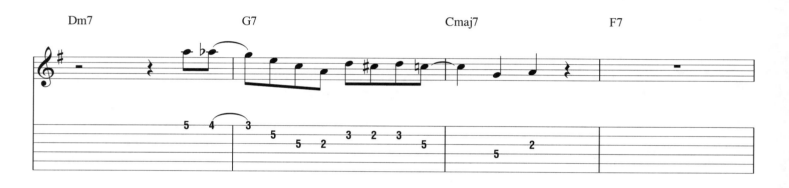

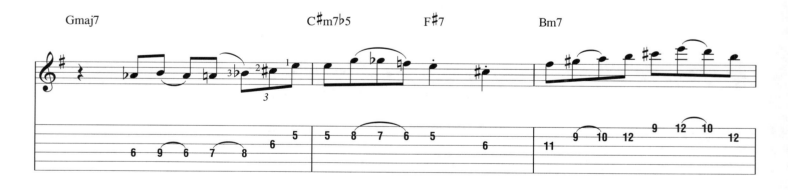

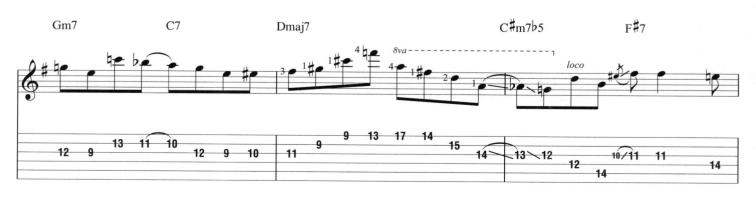

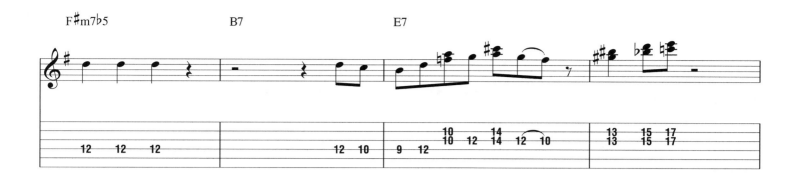

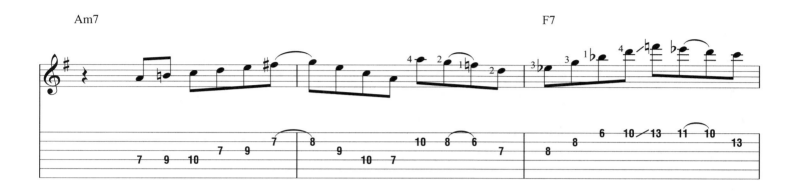

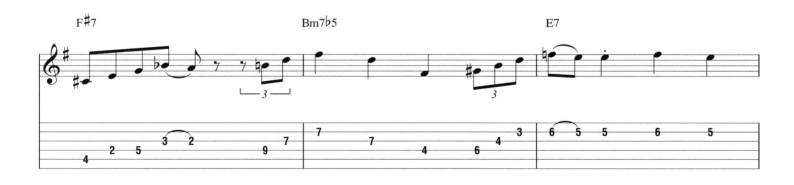

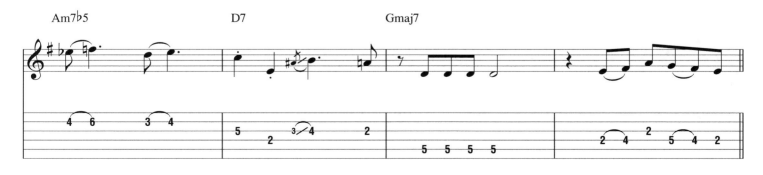

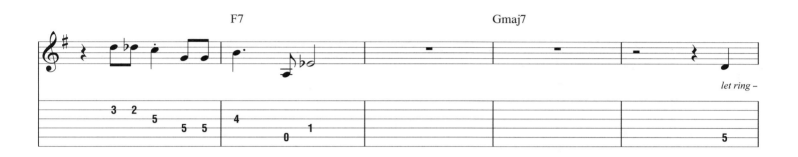

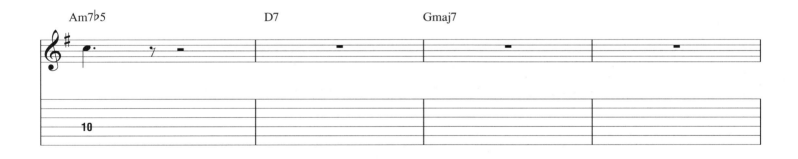

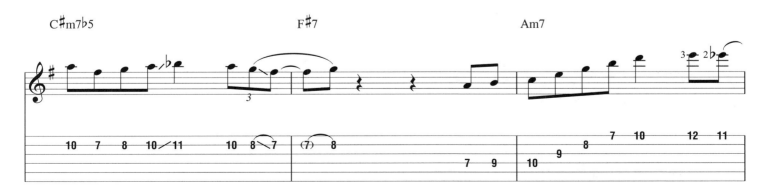

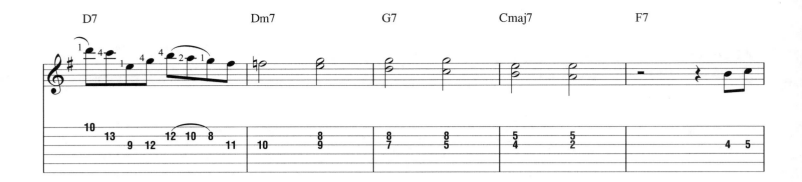

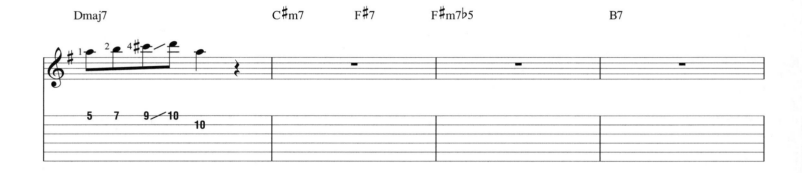

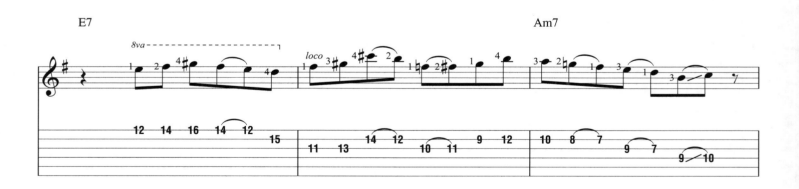

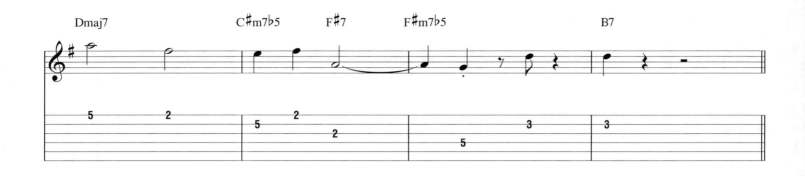

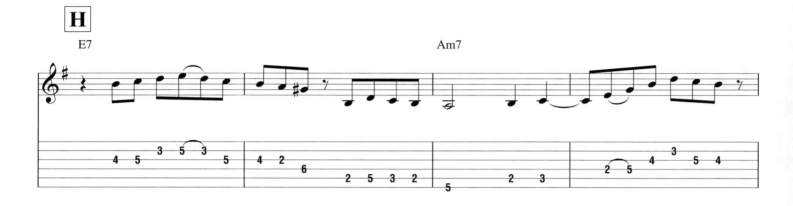

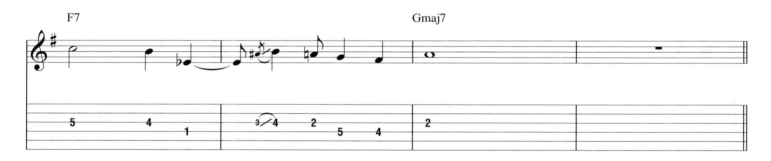

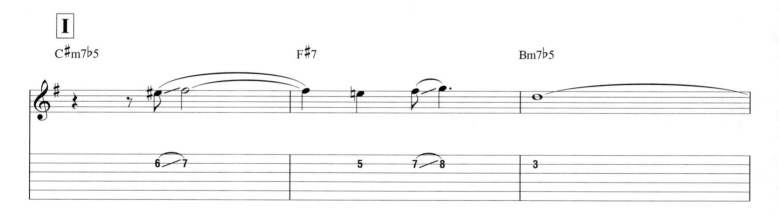

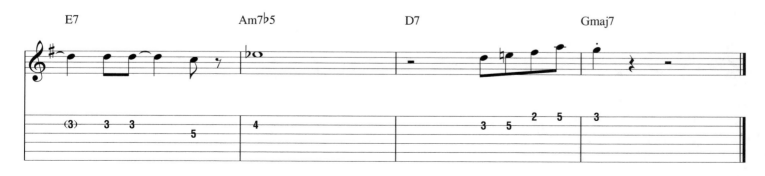

# Taking a Chance on Love

**Words by John La Touche and Ted Fetter**
**Music by Vernon Duke**

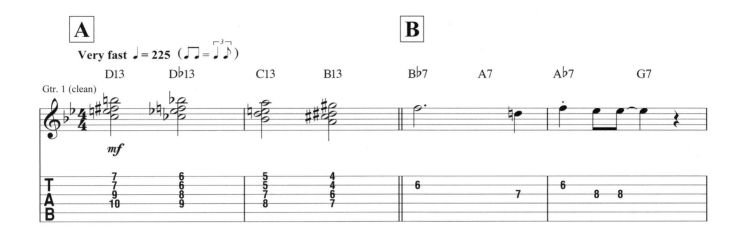

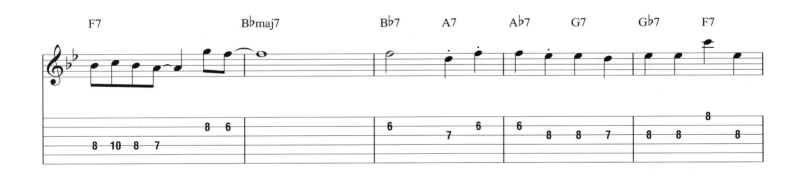

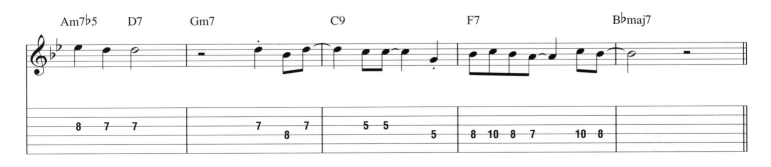

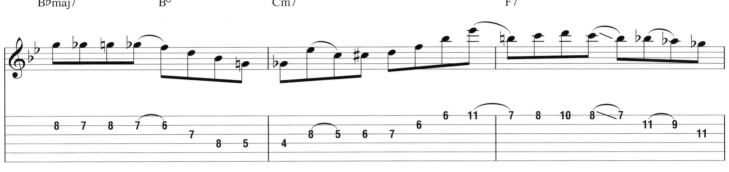

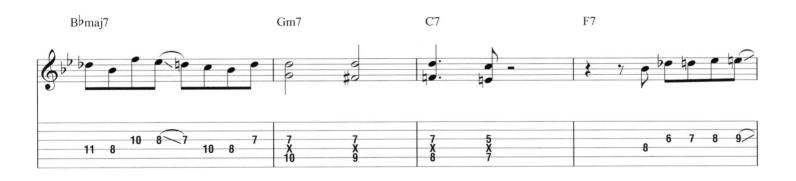

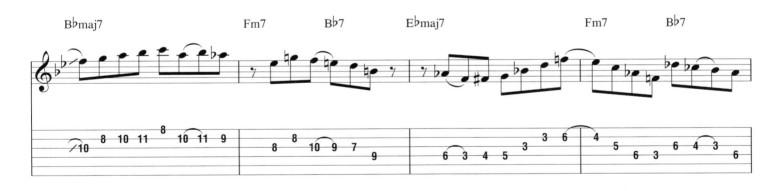

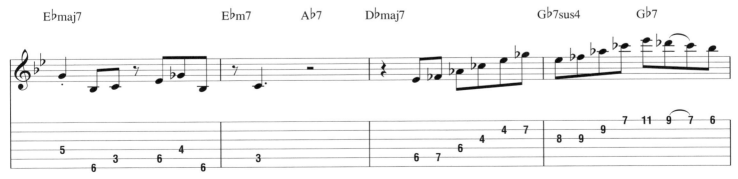

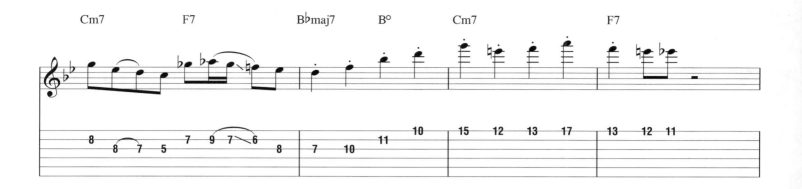

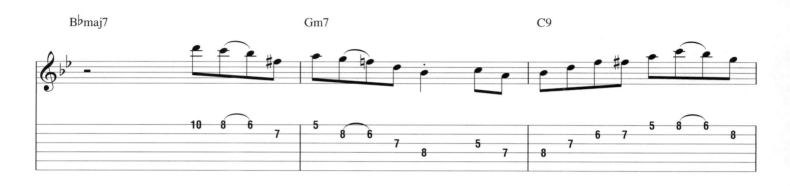

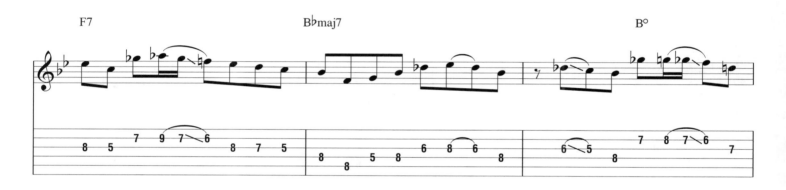

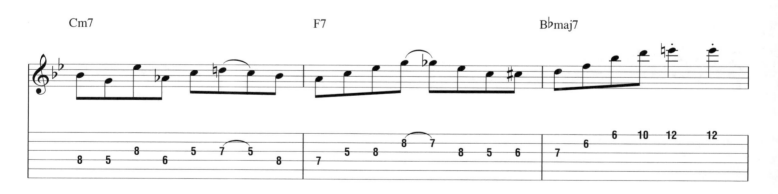

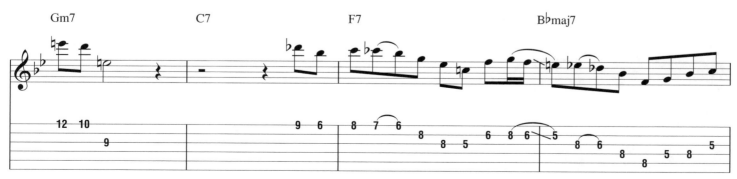

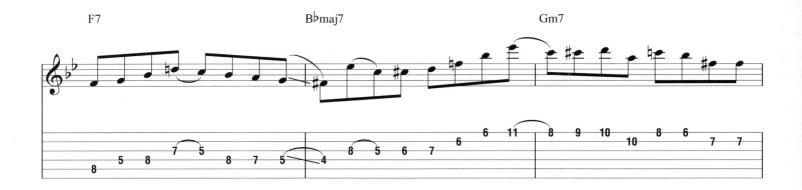

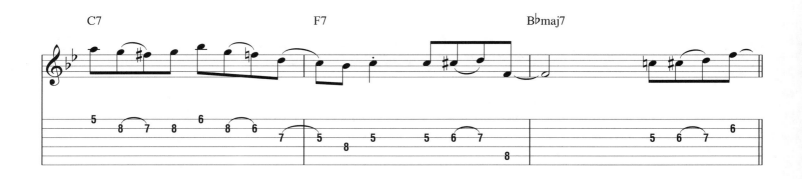

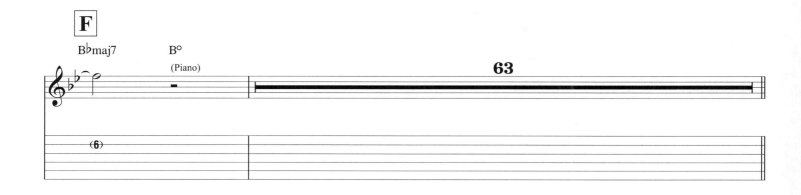

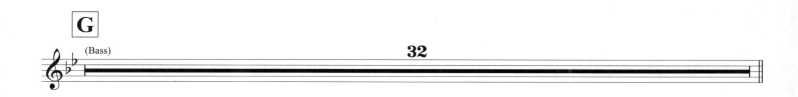

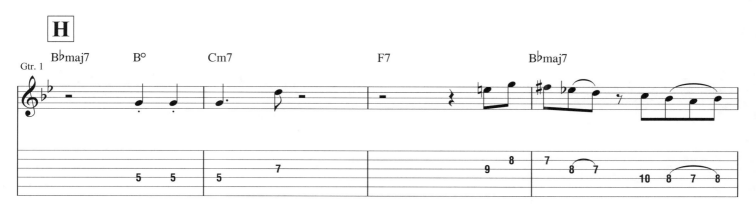

84

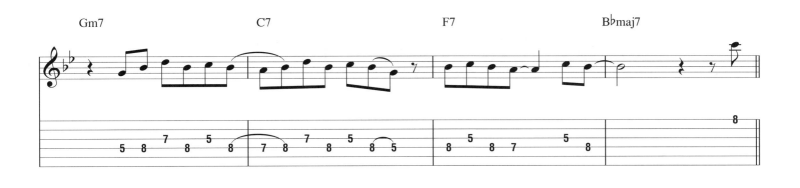

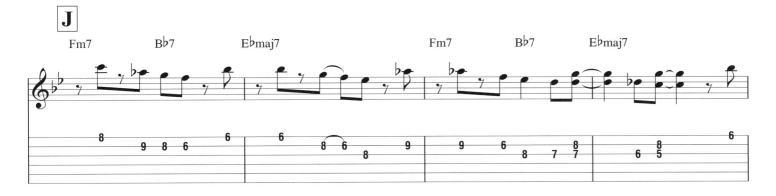

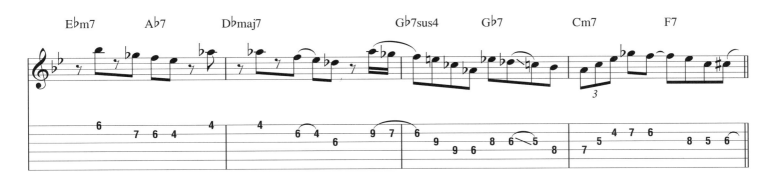

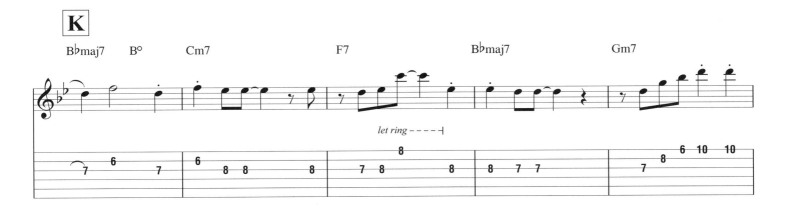

# There Is No Greater Love

**Words by Marty Symes**
**Music by Isham Jones**

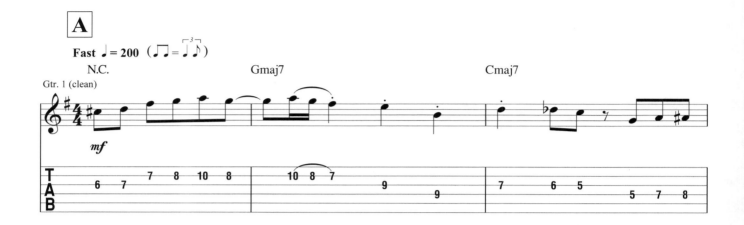

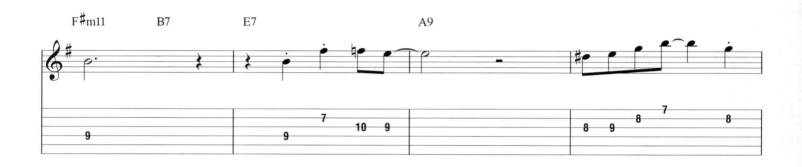

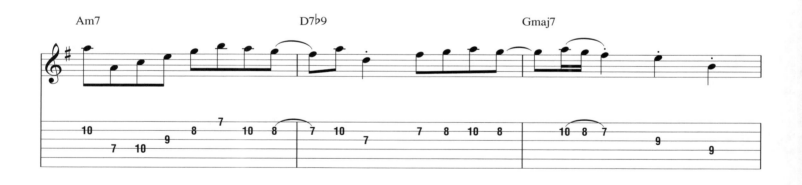

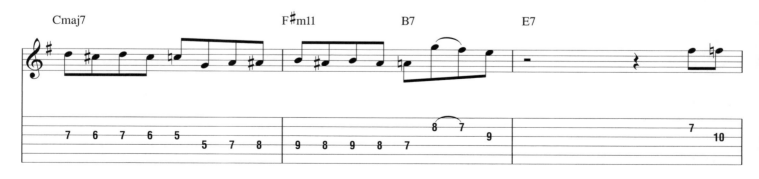

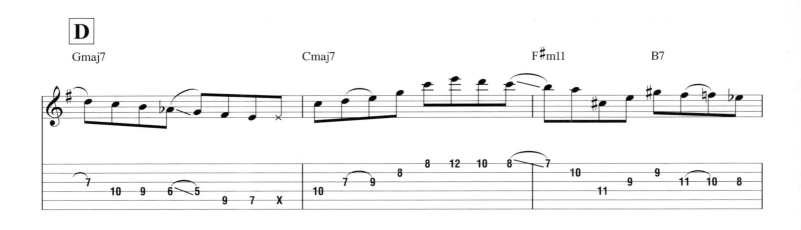

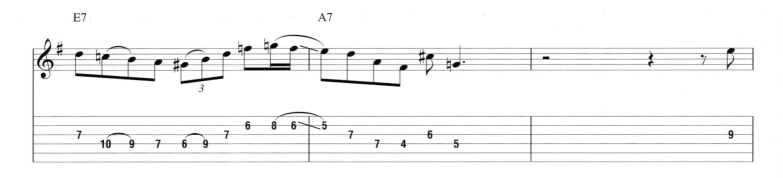

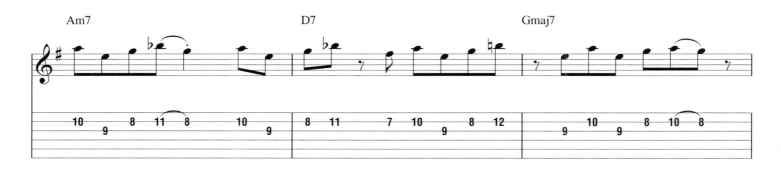

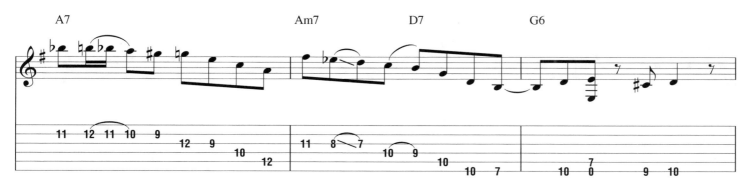

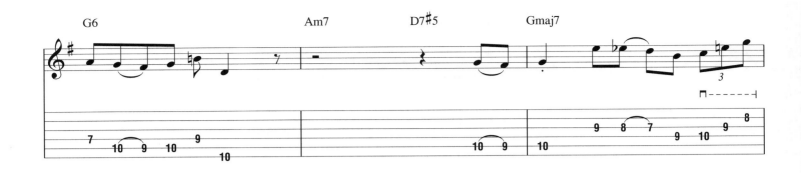

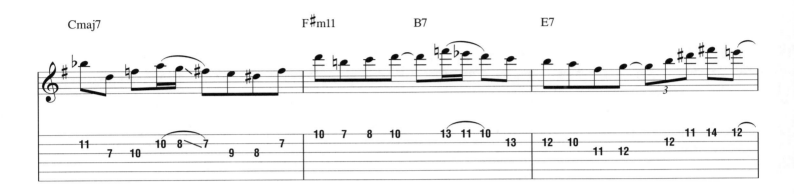

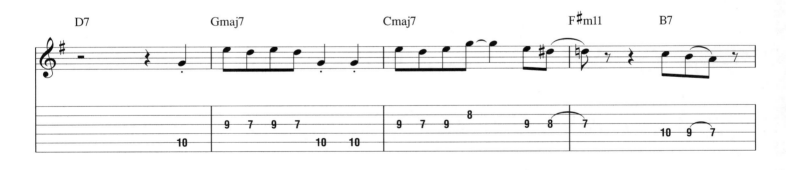

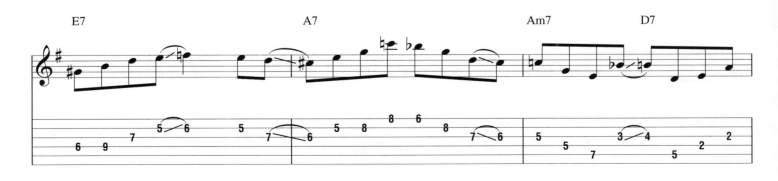

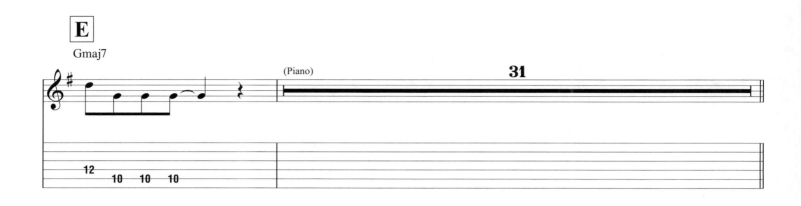

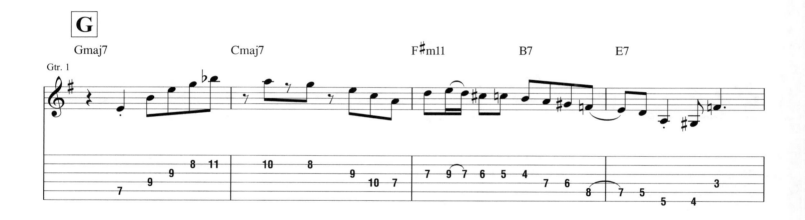

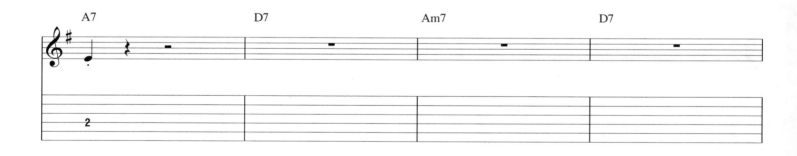

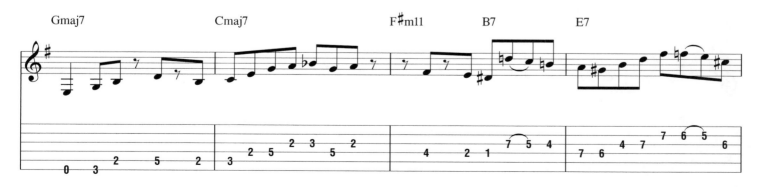

from *The Tal Farlow Album*

# You and the Night and the Music

**Words by Howard Dietz**
**Music by Arthur Schwartz**

*Chord symbols reflect overall harmony.

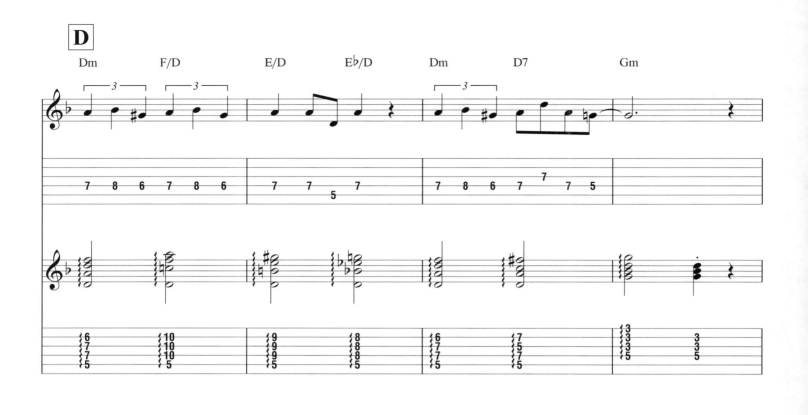

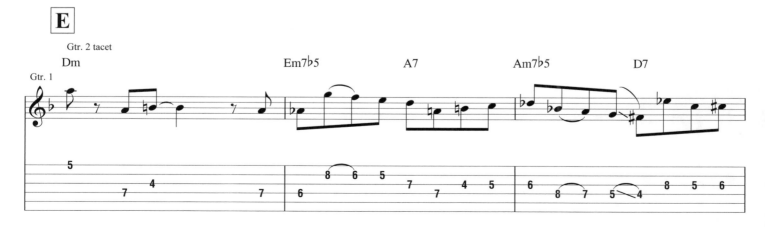

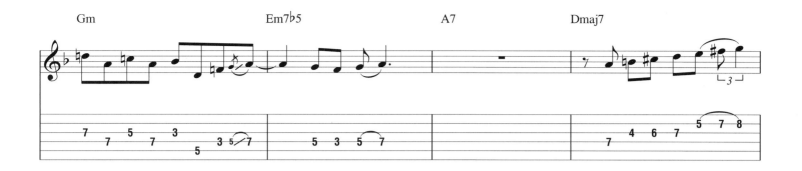

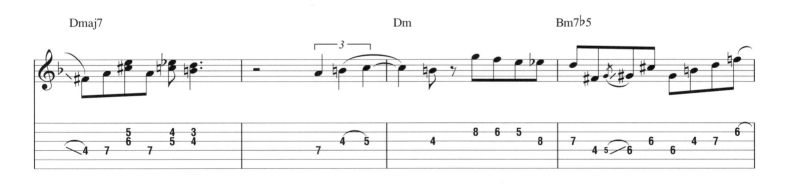

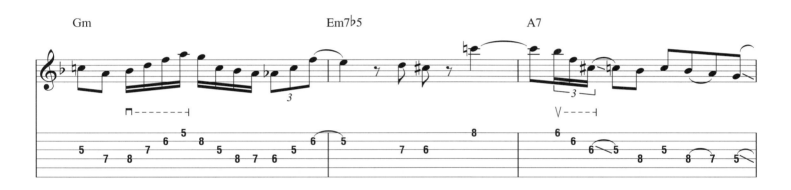

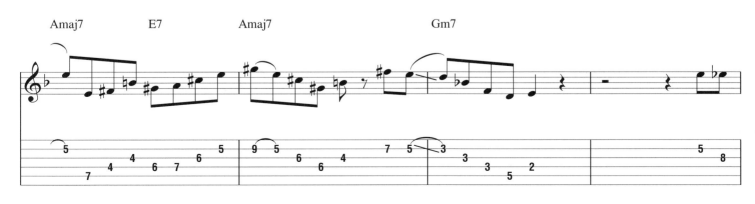

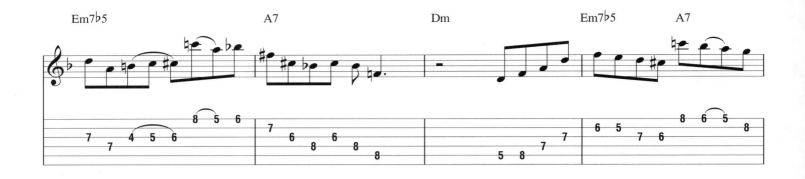

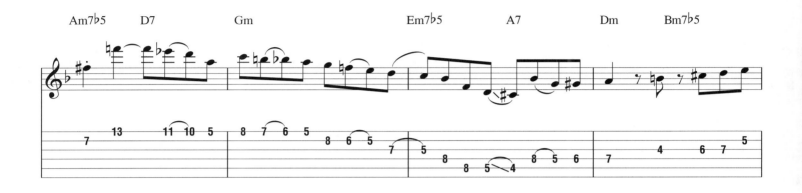

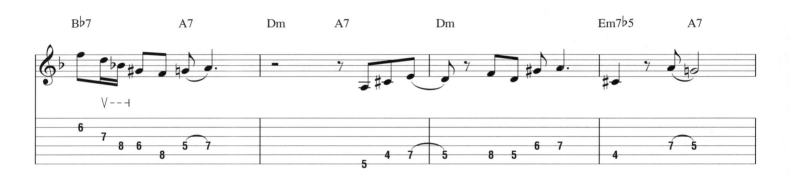

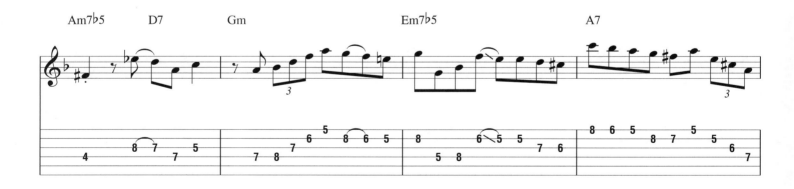

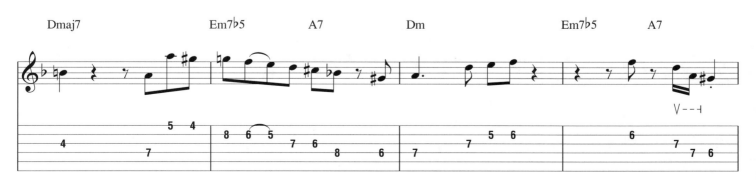

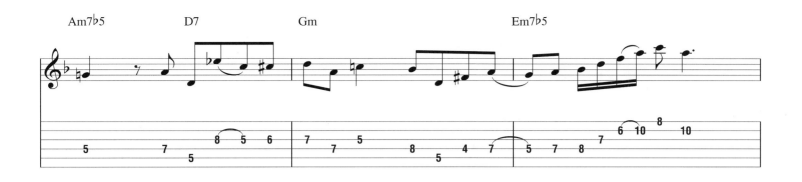

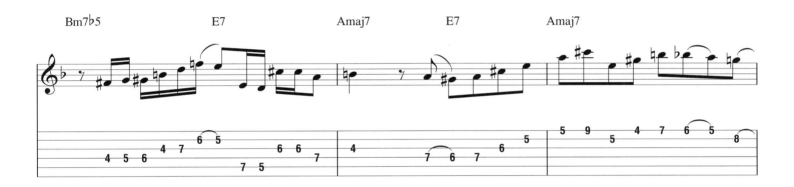

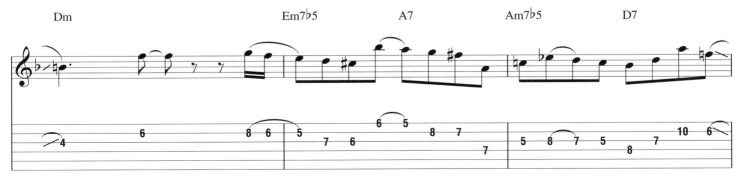

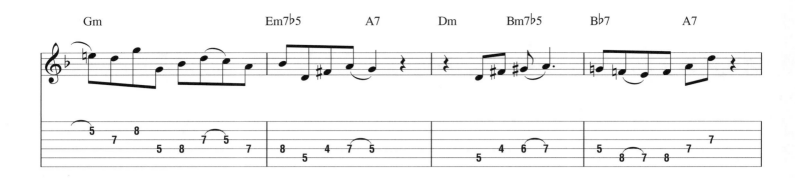

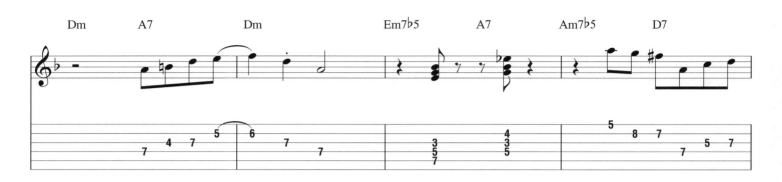

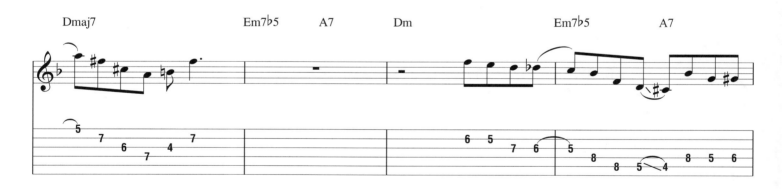

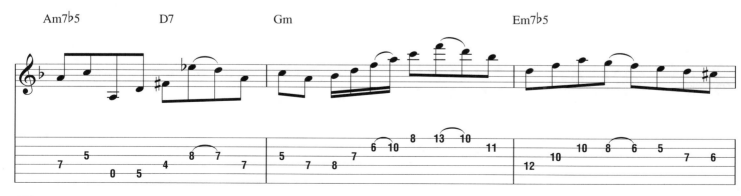

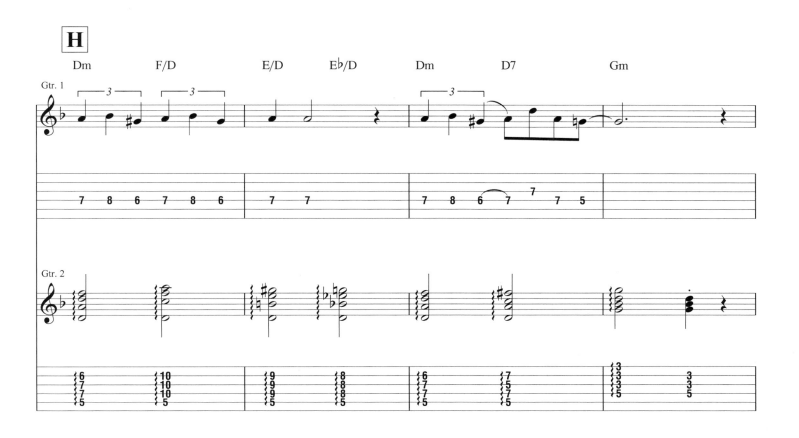

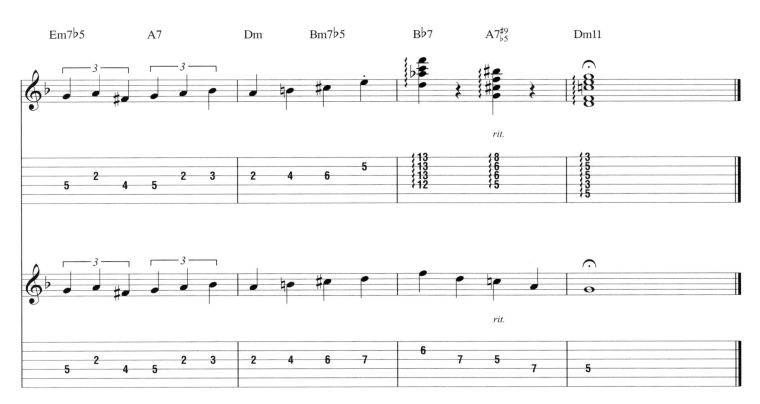

from *The Swinging Guitar of Tal Farlow*

# You Stepped Out of a Dream

from the M-G-M Picture ZIEGFELD GIRL

**Words by Gus Kahn**
**Music by Nacio Herb Brown**

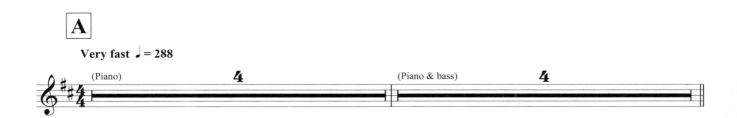

*Chord symbols reflect overall harmony.

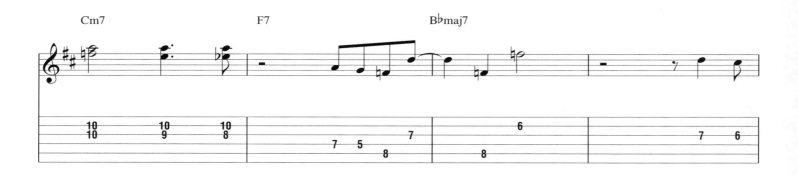

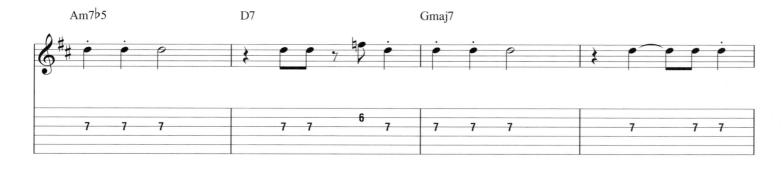

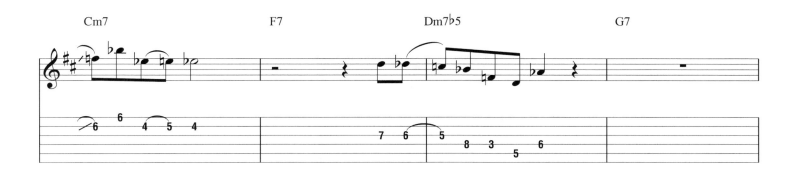

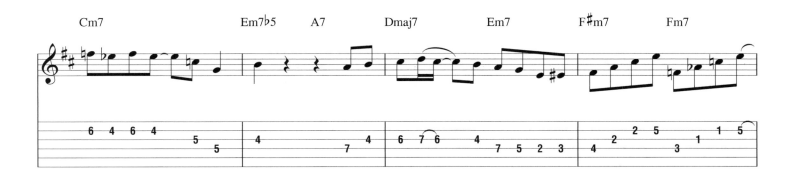

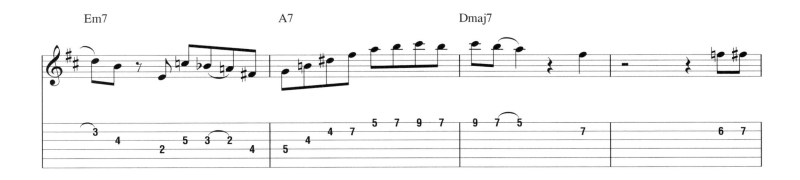

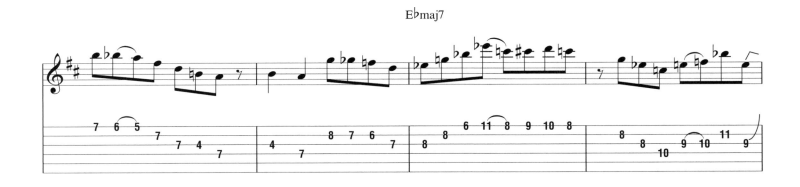

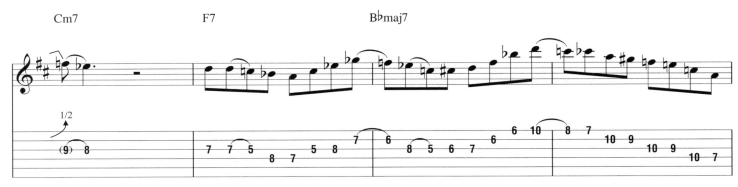

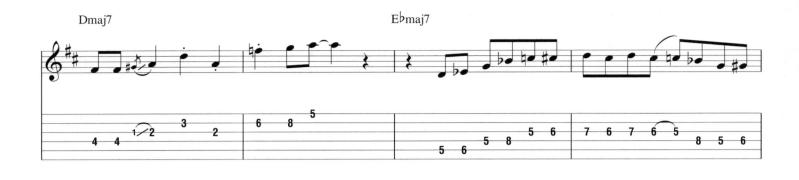

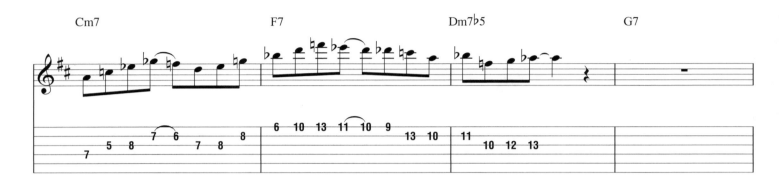

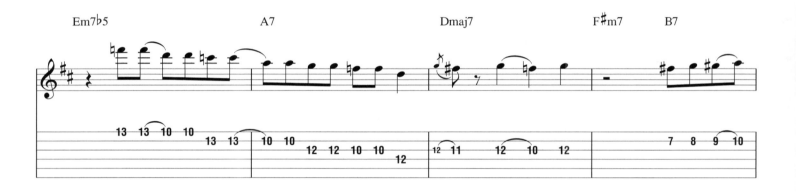

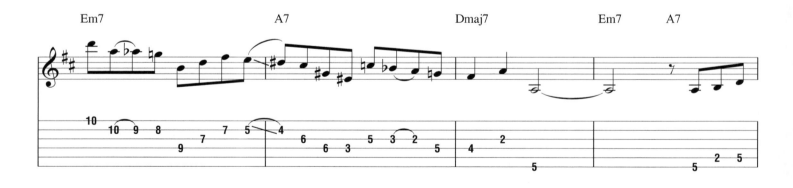

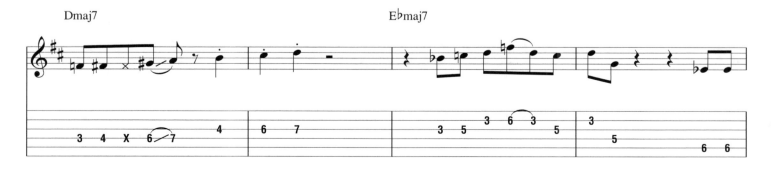

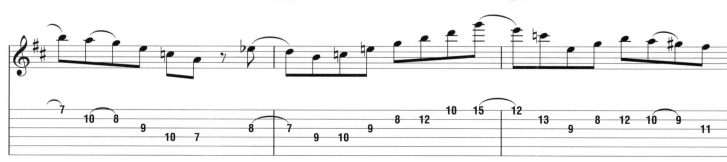

*Played behind the beat.

**Played ahead of the beat.

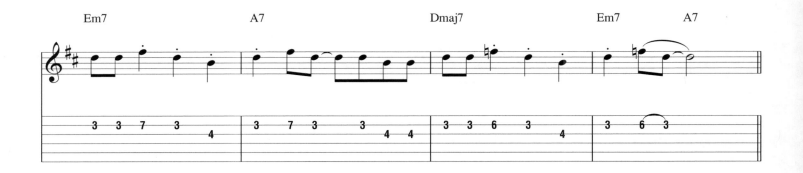

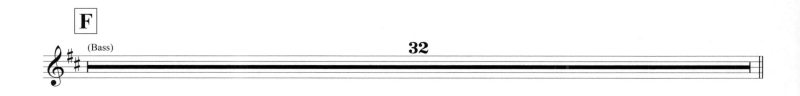

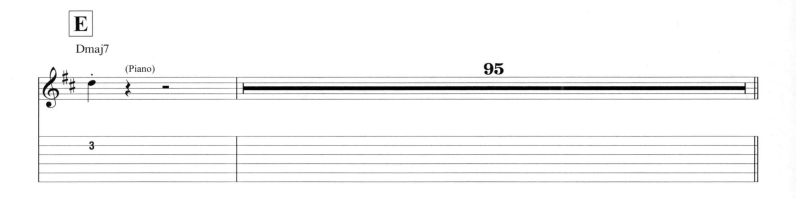

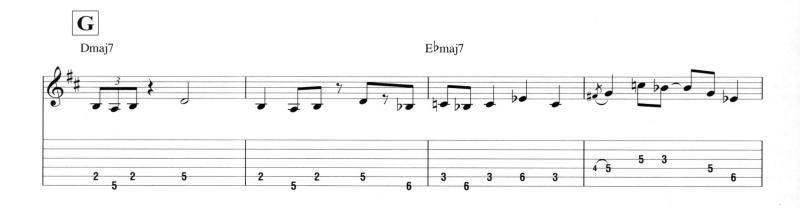

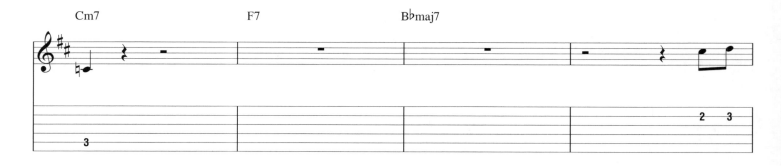

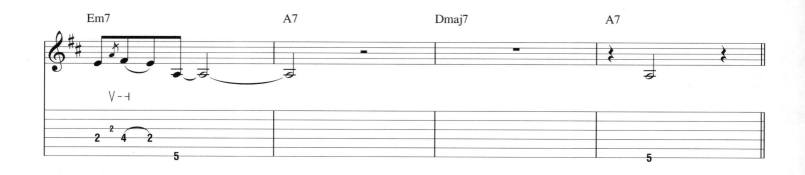

**H**

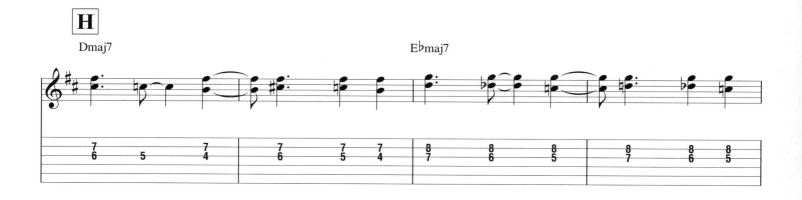

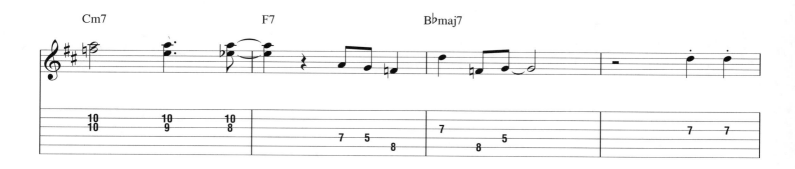

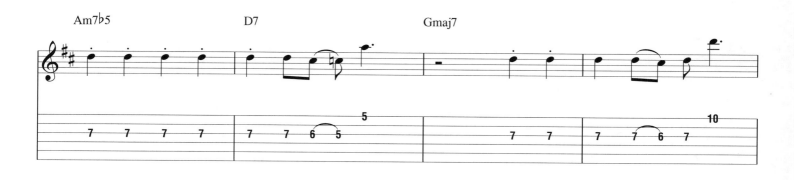

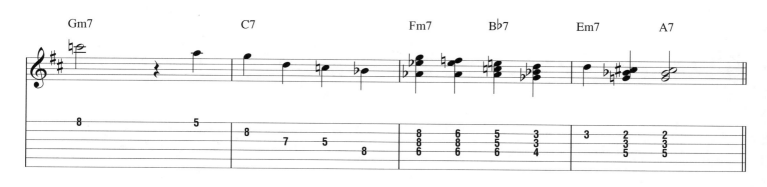

# You'd Be So Nice to Come Home To
## Words and Music by Cole Porter

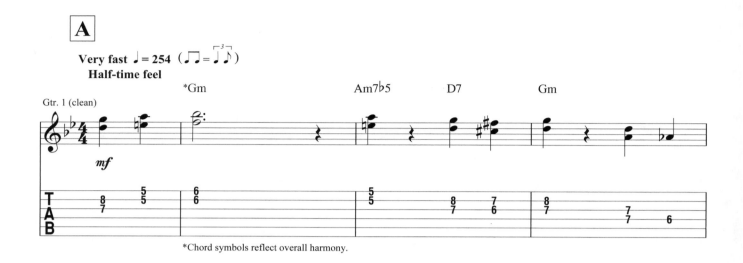

*Chord symbols reflect overall harmony.

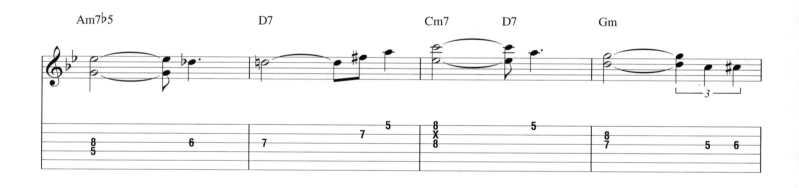

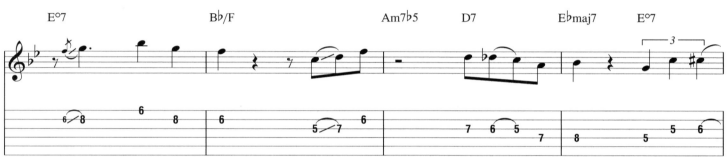

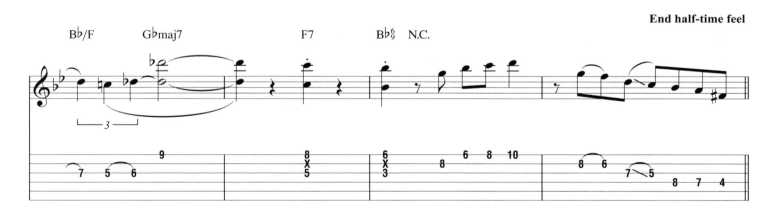

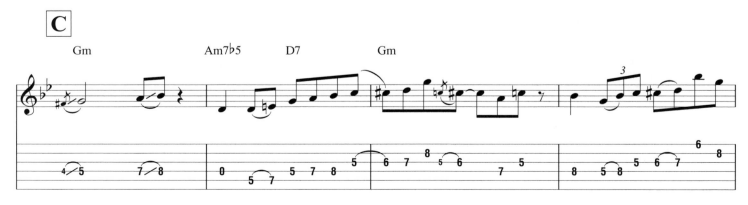

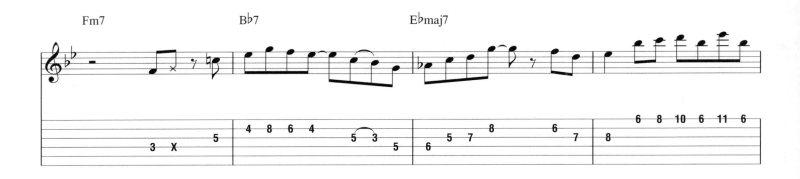

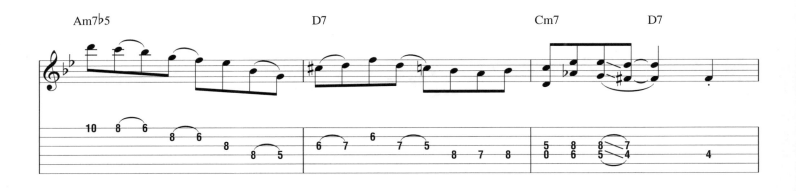

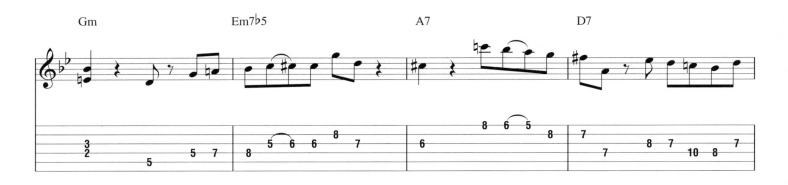

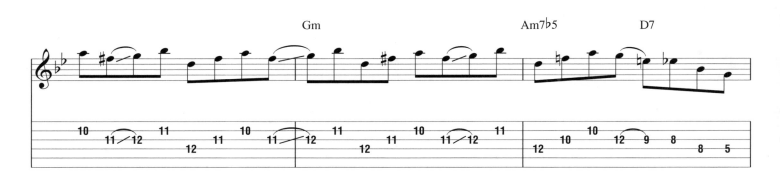

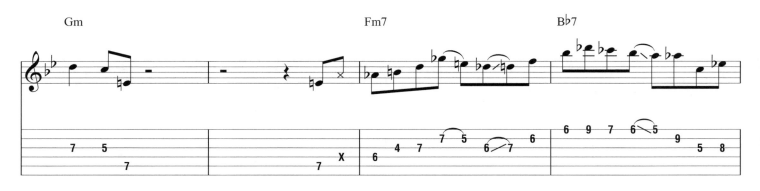

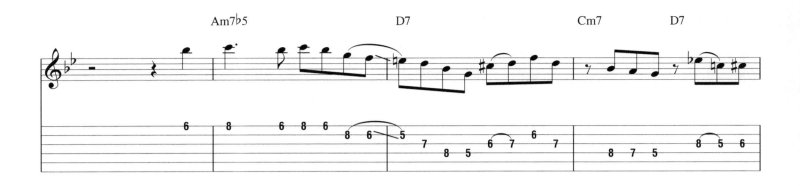

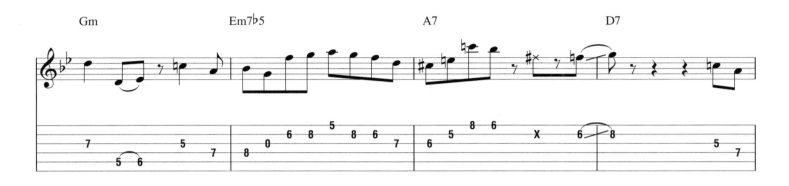

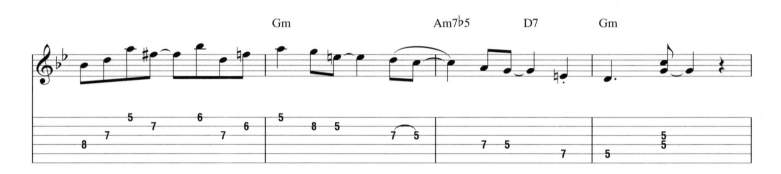

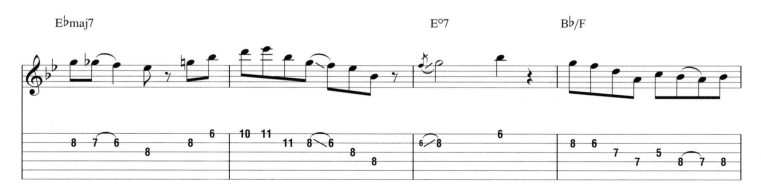

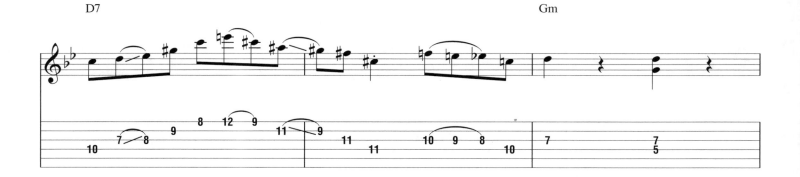

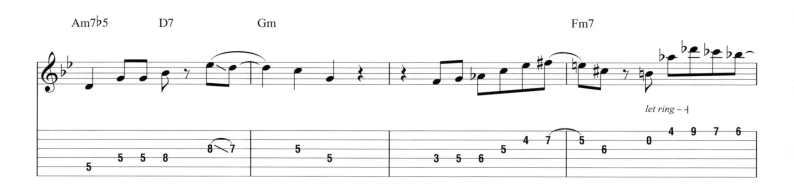

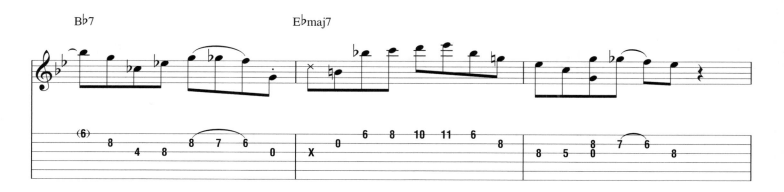

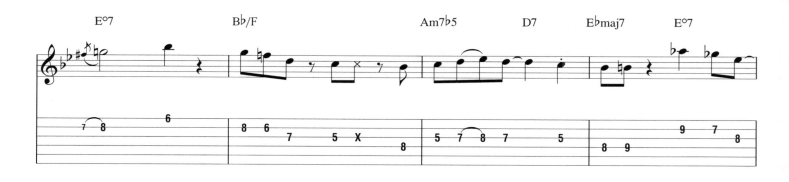

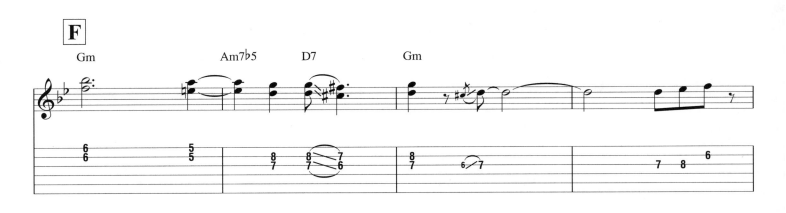

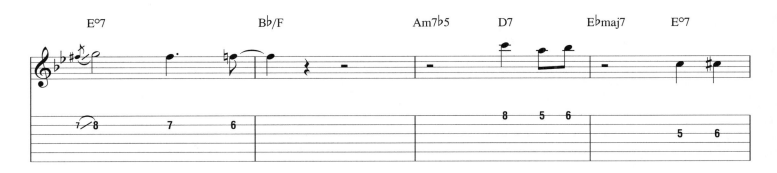

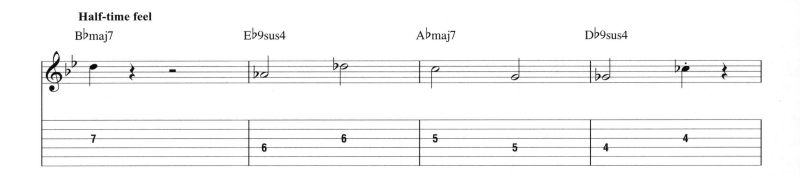

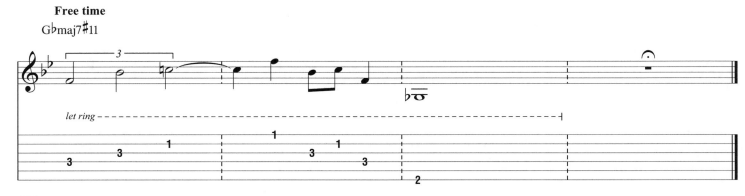